T

Beihefte zur Ökumenischen Rundschau Nr. 135

Mark Chapman | Matthias Grebe |
Friederike Nüssel | Frank-Dieter Fischbach (Eds.)

Towards Interchangeability

Reflections on Episcopacy in Theory and Practice

EVANGELISCHE VERLAGSANSTALT
Leipzig

Bibliographic information published by the Deutsche Nationalbibliothek
The Deutsche Nationalbibliothek lists this publication in the Deutsche
Nationalbibliographie; detailed bibliographic data are available on the
Internet at http://dnb.dnb.de.

This book is printed on ageing resistant paper.

Cover: Kai-Michael Gustmann, Leipzig
Typesetting: Steffi Glauche, Leipzig
Printing and Binding: Hubert & Co., Göttingen

ISBN 978-3-374-07123-4 // eISBN (PDF) 978-3-374-07124-1

www.eva-leipzig.de

Table of Contents

Introduction

Mark Chapman

The Meissen Theological Conference was to have been held at Ripon College, Cuddesdon, Oxfordshire in early July 2022. Because of the continuing effects of the coronavirus restrictions in both Germany and England and the difficulties of international transport, however, it had to be held online, which meant that many of the informal discussions over coffee and meals, which are so important in ecumenical relations, could not take place. Nevertheless, the meeting was able to build on the previous conference held in Hamburg in February 2019. Once again, it focused on the theme of oversight and ministry and how the remaining divisions between the Church of England and the EKD might be addressed constructively with a view to 'the full, visible unity of the body of Christ on earth'. This vision remains the intention of the Meissen Common Statement (III.7) and is at the heart of the Declaration itself (VI.17). One of the most interesting conclusions from the Hamburg Theological Conference was just how much there was still to explore about the nature and practice of episcopacy in the Church of England and the EKD despite the many efforts over the years.[1] Friederike Nüssel, the EKD co-chair of the Conference, and I, as Church of England co-chair, as well as the co-chairs of the Meissen Commission, Bishops Ralf Meister of Hanover and Jonathan Gibbs of Huddersfield, were consequently keen to continue this exploration by unpacking some of the key terms in which the remaining obstacles between the churches are framed and approaching them from different directions.

---

[1]   The papers were published in Mark Chapman, Friederike Nüssel and Matthias Grebe (eds), *Revisiting the Meissen Declaration after 30 Years* (Leipzig: Evangelische Verlagsanstalt, 2020).

To begin, it is worth remembering that the vast bulk of the Common Statement *On the Way to Visible Unity* of 18 March 1988[2] recognises a great degree of unity and even a common faith and tradition. Crucially, there is an acknowledgement that 'the Word of God is authentically preached and the sacraments of baptism and eucharist are duly administered' (VI.17.A.ii), words that are found in the formularies of both churches as constitutive of the church (CA7, Article 19). Alongside this is a mutual acknowledgement of 'an existing fidelity to the apostolic faith and mission, to the celebration of baptism and eucharist, and to the exercise of ordained ministries as given by God and instruments of his grace' (IV.12). Ministers are understood as 'given by God and instruments of his Grace' (VI.17.iii). In turn, both churches 'believe that a ministry of pastoral oversight (*episcopé*), exercised in personal, collegial and communal ways, is necessary to witness to and safeguard the unity and apostolicity of the Church' (V.15.viii). Similarly, in the Declaration (Section 17) the differing forms of episcopé are understood 'as a visible sign of the Church's unity and continuity in apostolic life, mission and ministry' (iv), even though such episcopé is somewhat cryptically referred to as sometimes non-episcopal, by which is presumably meant that it is exercised in ways other than simply by bishops.

Despite these high levels of agreement, however, the interchangeability of ministers remains impossible for the Church of England. The Preface to the Church of England's Ordinal of 1662 made it seemingly clear that 'No man shall be accounted or taken to be a lawful Bishop, Priest, or Deacon in the Church of England, or suffered to execute any of the said functions, except he be called, tried, examined, and admitted thereunto, according to the Form hereafter following, or hath had formerly Episcopal Consecration or Ordination'. This emphasis on episcopal ordination according to a certain form meant that despite the unity already shared, the appointment of clergy from the EKD could not be taken to be lawful within the Church of England. This is emphasised by the injunctions against concelebration in a footnote to the Declaration, as well as forbidding some forms of symbolic action such as the laying on of hands by a Church of England bishop at an ordination in one of the member churches of the EKD. The crucial paragraph of the Common Statement which expresses these differences is at V.16:

---

[2]   The Agreement is at: https://www.churchofengland.org/media/3320 (accessed 21 March 2022).

Lutheran, Reformed and United Churches, though being increasingly prepared to appreciate episcopal succession as a sign of the apostolicity of the life of the whole Church, hold that this particular form of *episkope* should not become a necessary condition for "full, visible unity". The Anglican understanding of full, visible unity includes the historic episcopate and full interchangeability of ministers. Because of this remaining difference our mutual recognition of one another's ministries does not yet result in the full interchangeability of ministers.

If there were to be any hope of moving further towards 'full, visible unity' it consequently seemed imperative to us to revisit this remaining obstacle and to seek fresh ways of investigating some of the most contested areas, most obviously what may or may not be meant by 'historic episcopate' and 'episcopal succession'. These phrases are used in the Common Statement but are somewhat different from the phrasing of the Book of Common Prayer Ordinal which mentions neither 'historic' not 'succession'. Our approach was to start from the grass roots. While most of the earlier Meissen Theological Conferences have necessarily focused on episcopacy, what has been remarkably underexplored is how episcopacy has been *practised* both in the present day and in the past. It has usually been discussed as a doctrinal and systematic question rather than being approached from the perspective of *practical* theology. The questions raised are simple: is the term 'historic episcopate' open to a variety of practical interpretations? Is it feasible for Anglicans to imagine a version of 'full, visible unity' that does not require either the 'historic episcopate' or the 'full interchangeability of ministers'?

Although official ecumenists appointed by their churches must obviously work within the constraints of texts as well as accepting their representative role, there is also a sense in which all texts have to be reread and re-interpreted in the light of new questions that might be taken to them. Part of our efforts to reinvigorate the work of the Meissen Theological Conference has been to resource the conversations of the Commission and to experiment with new ways of approaching 'full, visible unity' in the contemporary context. After all, the changes of the past 34 years have been profound in our churches. In 1988, for instance, the ministry of the Church of England was very different from today: most obviously, there were no women priests and neither were there Provincial Episcopal Visitors – the so-called 'flying bishops' who minister to those clergy and parishes that have voted not to allow women to minister. From 1994, intercommunion *within* the Church of England has been compromised, and with the advent of women bishops things have changed still further: not all those ordained according to the rites of the Church of England and by bishops of the Church of England can minister in every parish within that church. While this specific issue did not feature among the papers presented at the Conference in 2021, it was no doubt in the background of some of the Church of England contributions. It raises new questions: what does this present situation say about the nature of the 'historic episcopate'? Is it any more anomalous than it would be to allow those EKD clergy to minister in the Church of England, especially given that their orders have already been recognised as conveying grace?

However, rather than addressing such questions head-on, the Conference took as its starting point a number of examples of episcopacy as practised and how far it could be understood as uniform and consistent. The short phrase 'historic episcopate' has frequently been used as if it has an obvious and uncontested meaning, but it is not clear that this is the case. The intention behind the conference was consequently to begin to interrogate the meaning of the term in all its complexity both through history and in the present. We consequently asked the contributors the following questions: how has episcopacy functioned at different moments in the life of the church? And how does this inform the practice of episcopacy today? Such questions require the study of local and particular expressions of oversight and how these have striven to maintain the apostolic 'historic' faith both explicitly or implicitly. Indeed, one might ask, if the traditional notion of 'apostolic faith' as used in many ecumenical texts is taken to involve a *historic* dimension and makes historical claims, it could perhaps function as a terminological bridge to understand the 'historic episcopate' as a means for preserving the historic apostolic faith, which might not require a 'personal' expression of such a historical episcopate (as several of the papers from the German contributors emphasize).

The papers presented at the conference revealed a huge range of understandings of *episcope* as it has been practised. Indeed, the papers soon revealed that the idea of a uniform 'historic episcopate' which has remained identical through history is little more than wishful thinking. Morwenna Ludlow, for instance, addressed the topic from the perspective of the Cappadocian Fathers of the early church and Frances Knight discussed episcopacy in the very different context of the mid-nineteenth century in the massive Church of England diocese of Lincoln. From the German perspective, Bernd Oberdorfer discussed the rise of personal episcopacy in relation to synodality from 1918 through a period of enormous change and political turmoil. From a more doctrinal perspective Friederike Nüssel discussed apostolicity and historic succession from a Lutheran perspective, again nuancing the idea of 'historic episcopate'. Similarly, Peter Scherle investigated the rites of ordination in the EKD and in the Church of England, which for Anglicans raises obvious questions about the the Preface to the Book of Common Prayer in its talk of the 'form' of the ordinal. Each of these papers consequently raises significant questions about the meaning of the letter of the Common Statement.

In addition to a detailed discussion of the practice of episcopacy through history, several of our contributors were able to reflect on the practice of episcopacy in their own experience. The changing status of authority and power in modern constitutional settlements has profoundly altered the conceptions of sovereignty and consent. Indeed, one might ask: how does the exercise of authority in modern democratic societies relate to the sort of authority claimed by bishops who had earlier exercised a jurisdiction that was dependent on pre-modern forms of governance and political and social authority? In this context, Ralf Meister, as Bishop of Hanover and lead bishop of the VELKD (United Evangelical Lutheran Church of Germany) was able to reflect on the kind of authority embodied in the office of the Bishop which was as much a function of status and position in civil society as an office in the church: while in Germany there might be complete separation between church and state in law, this does not mean that the bishop lacks status and authority. Such soft authority obviously deeply affects the way in which episcopacy functions. Alex Hughes similarly drew on his own experience as archdeacon with formal duties of oversight but as part of a collective expression of episcopacy. How this is perceived on the ground, however, proves to be very different from how it might be conceived in theory. This was particularly true when hard decisions have to be made against the shrinking financial resources of the church.

Immediately before the Theological Conference the members of the Meissen Commission from the Church of England side organised an online Meissen-led Colloquium for ecumenical guests, where members of other denominations were asked to reflect on the understanding of 'identity' both in relation to episcopacy and more generally. This led to very fruitful discussions which helped inform the debate in the Conference. Miriam Haar's contribution to this volume was developed from her brief contribution. The paper by Matthias Grebe and Jonathan Gibbs outlines some of the salient points as well as pointing to possible future directions for discussion in the Meissen Commission.

One other area needs mentioning. In one of its bold and aspirational claims, the Common Statement suggests that 'In order to fulfil its mission the Church itself must be united. It is within a missionary perspective that we can begin to overcome the divisions which have kept us apart' (III.6). This is evidently related to the changing missional context of both churches. While the Church of England's ministry has changed significantly since 1988, the Church itself has also declined rapidly in terms of membership and resources, both human and financial. Easter Communicants have dropped from about 3 per cent of the population in 1988 to about 1.7 per cent in 2019, which is roughly in line with the drop in membership rolls. Infant baptisms have collapsed to about 8 per cent of births in 2019 compared with 28.9 per cent in 1987. Although the bi-confessional nature of German society makes comparisons complicated, membership of the EKD churches is far higher than that of the Church of England, as is the baptism rate, even though both have declined since 1988. Changing demography both within society and church raises quite different questions from the late Cold War context of 1988: the 'missionary perspective' is now far more urgent in a situation of rapid decline. For this reason, it is possible that the securities of the past where identities were fixed around such markers as the 'historic episcopate' and particular confessions are no longer as relevant as they might once have been. Ecumenical co-operation and collaboration both within nation states and across national boundaries consequently becomes increasingly pressing.

My own paper sought to explore this issue obliquely by discussing the background to the development of the Church of South India which raised many of the same issues over the question of the role of the historic episcopate in the identity of the church. The missionary situation made the historic divisions between the denominations in the Indian sub-continent quite irrelevant when set against the broader context of Indian society. While the final agreement which led to the establishment of the Church of South India meant that all new clergy would be ordained by bishops standing in the Anglican episcopal succession, there was nonetheless an anomaly that allowed non-episcopally-ordained ministers to serve in the new Church of South India in the interim period. It was this anomaly that provoked enormous opposition among Anglo-Catholics in England. An ecclesial identity that had been invested in the historic episcopate was set against the unification of a divided church in a missionary context. Furthermore, some Anglicans at the time even sought a different form of unity that could allow for very different models of oversight in different places: this raises the question of how far the exigencies of mission trump questions of doctrinal purity. Recent experience of Church of England ecumenism with British Methodists reveals the continued influence of an identity established on the 'historic episcopate': unity would have required a similar 'bearable anomaly' to that of South India which meant that the proposals failed to gain traction in General Synod, not least among its House of Bishops.

What all this means is that the quest for full, visible unity remains both highly contested and highly problematic. To jump over the remaining hurdles will require something that to many in the Church of England would look like a suspension of the Preface to the Ordinal and a sacrifice of its ecclesial identity. Nuanced explanation of the meaning of 'historic episcopate' might undoubtedly help in illuminating something of the context of the two churches and remove some misunderstandings; but among those for whom it remains a visceral aspect of ecclesial identity such arguments are unlikely to be convincing. Perhaps more plausible as a way forward into the future is an emphasis on the importance of bearing anomalies for the sake of mission (which are to a limited extent already recognised in the ecumenical canons of the Church of England). From the German perspective it is also possible to imagine the possibility of a limited degree of acceptance of what Anglicans like to call the 'gift of Episcopacy', perhaps deriving from those bishops in the Nordic countries who are in communion with both the Church of England and the EKD and who might function as a bridge from one to the other. Yet in a polity as diverse as that of the EKD, which is as much of a communion of churches as it is a church, this too might be too much of an anomaly to bear if it became a *necessary* condition for the ordination of ministers. But, we might ask, could it become a universal practice even if it were not absolutely necessary? Perhaps, then, both churches might need to rethink how the historic faith is to be transmitted to the next generation and what form of oversight is necessary to make that happen. In a world where the survival of the apostolic faith itself is at stake, the quest for full, visible unity becomes increasingly urgent. It might mean that the future shape of the 'historic episcopate' might take a form very different from what any of us might imagine.

Feast of the Annunciation, 25 March 2022

The scope and limits of episcopal collaboration in fourth century Cappadocia

The soul of the city and the body of Christ

Morwenna Ludlow

> May our invitation not be in vain, by which we invite you now
> to visit our city .... deign to come to us without hesitation, and
> to anticipate the days of the synod so that we may converse at
> leisure with each other and be mutually encouraged through the
> communion of spiritual gifts.
>
> Basil, *Letter* 176, to Bishop Amphilochius of Iconium[1]

I. Introduction

In the year 374, Basil of Caesarea, the great defender of Nicene Christianity, influential bishop and monastic organiser, wrote to a younger colleague,
Amphilochius, asking him to visit for a few days before the beginning of a
church synod. They could celebrate together the annual local festival of
the martyrs. They could talk. But there lies a tension in his invitation.
Echoing Romans 1:12–13, Basil declares his need for the mutual encouragement which Amphilochius' presence would bring to them both, but he
also indicates his own seniority: there is a clear sense that his invitation is
a summons, fitting the fact that Amphilochius is his spiritual 'true son'.[2]

In this brief paper I will sketch out a picture of the practical workings
of *episcope* in the fourth century, using Cappadocia as my case-study. In
particular I will offer some reflections on the question: what were the opportunities for and limits to bishops' collaboration in their episcopal vocation? In the first main section (II.), I address this question from the perspective of an overview of the institutional framework of fourth-century

---

[1] Basil, *Letters*, trans. Roy J. Deferrari, Loeb Classical Library (London; Cambridge,
Mass: Heinemann; Harvard UP, 1926), 459.

[2] Basil, *Letter* 176, tr. Deferrari, 459. Romans 1:12-13: 'For I am longing to see you
so that I may share with you some spiritual gift to strengthen you – or rather so
that we may be mutually encouraged by each other's faith, both yours and mine.'

episcopacy (looking briefly, for example, at the role of the metropolitan and the 'area' or 'country' bishops). In the next section (III.), I offer two specific examples of the ways in which fourth-century Cappadocian bishops worked in collaborative projects and for mutual support. My particular focus will be Basil of Caesarea, partly because of his role as metropolitan, and partly because of the usefulness of his extensive extant correspondence as evidence.

II. Bishops, metropolitans and area bishops in the fourth century Roman province

1. Structures

Christian bishops in this period were appointed to cities (rather than to a precisely-designated geographical region like the modern diocese), although each city naturally had influence over a surrounding rural area. As we shall see, some of these cities were very small indeed. By the fourth century, there was a clear expectation that the bishop of the administrative capital of a province would have pastoral oversight over the clergy (bishops, priests and deacons) of that whole province.[3] In particular, he had to ratify the appointment of any bishop in the province.[4] Thus, when in 370 Basil was consecrated bishop of Caesarea, the administrative capital of Cappadocia, he rightly expected to exercise ecclesiastical oversight over the clergy throughout the province of Cappadocia. When Valens divided the province in two in 372, Basil was less than pleased to find an episcopal colleague Anthimus exercising oversight over the new Province of Cappadocia Secunda in virtue of being bishop of Tyana, the new Provincial Capital. Basil retained oversight over clergy in Cappadocia Prima and attempted to repair his reduced influence by creating new episcopal posts.

---

[3]   Technically, ecclesiastical structures mapped on to provinces and their cities. The term 'diocese' originally referred to a much larger Roman imperial administrative unit: in the fourth century the Roman Empire consisted of four Prefectures (Gallia, Italica, Illyricum, Oriens), and around twelve 'Dioceses' (the number changed according to various administrative reforms). The geographical area of Asia Minor, for example, consisted of two Dioceses: Asiana to the west and Pontica to the east. The province of Cappadocia was one of the seven provinces making up the diocese of Pontica.

[4]   4th Canon of the Council of Nicaea, the first recorded use of the term 'metropolitan': Bradley K. Storin and Oliver Nicholson, 'Metropolitan', in *The Oxford Dictionary of Late Antiquity*, ed. Oliver Nicholson (Oxford University Press, 2018).

Notoriously, he consecrated his brother Gregory of Nyssa and his friend Gregory of Nazianzus bishops of Nyssa and Sasima respectively – towns which were tiny, but strategically sited on the borders of Cappadocia Prima and Cappadocia Secunda.[5] Neither Gregory was pleased and Gregory of Nazianzus never visited Sasima![6]

One consequently finds in the fourth century a network of bishops of various cities, large and small. Each bishop 'looked up' to an ecclesiastical superior, the 'metropolitan', in the provincial capital. In turn, the metropolitan bishops of certain major cities in the Roman Empire, namely Rome, Alexandria, Antioch and Constantinople exerted ecclesiastical influence over a much wider region. The 6th Canon of Nicaea is evidence of a growing understanding of a group of provinces (e.g. Egypt, Libya and Cyrenaica) being under the influence of one bishop and his church (in this case, Alexandria). However, even by the late fourth century this influence was not clearly systematised: it operated differently in different regions and authority was frequently contested.[7]

Each bishop of a city worked with a group of local priests under his oversight – both in the city and in the surrounding area. In small towns like Nyssa, for example, a bishop's duties might largely look, to modern eyes, like those of a priest in charge of a benefice working as the most senior member of a team of priests and deacons. Bishops were required to travel and, since travel was time-consuming, at least one priest was required *in situ* to carry out regular liturgical duties. Although some deacons and priests travelled on church business (sometimes as messengers for their bishops), many did not. Basil remarks that 'even if our clergy seems to be numerous, yet it is composed of men who are unpractised in travel, because they do not travel for business nor follow out-of-doors occupations, but generally practise the sedentary arts, deriving therefrom the means for their daily livelihood'.[8] His complaint is not an ideological ranking of a more politically-engaged / active over an ascetic approach to Christian vocation; rather, he is simply worried about sending inexperienced trav-

---

5   For this episode see e.g. Philip Rousseau, *Basil of Caesarea* (Berkeley, CA: Univ of California Pr, 1998), 235–39; John McGuckin, *St Gregory of Nazianzus: An Intellectual Biography* (Crestwood NY: St Vladimir's Seminary Press, 2001), chap. 4.
6   Rousseau, *Basil of Caesarea*, 235.
7   Storin and Nicholson, 'Metropolitan'. It was the later Council of Chalcedon (451) which formalised the appeal 'from the decisions of a metropolitan to the *exarch*, the bishop of the principal city of a (civil) *diocesis*'.
8   Seemingly referring to his priests' previous occupations. Basil, *Letter* 198.1 (tr. adapted from Deferrari's Basil, *Letters*, 101. See Rousseau, *Basil of Caesarea*, 152.

ellers out on roads which had been 'closed until Easter' due to a severe winter.[9]

Travel, and therefore communication, in a largely rural region like Cappadocia was a constant problem. (In the letter just cited, Basil apologises to his addressee for a gap in their communication: letters were delayed due to Basil not knowing anyone travelling in the right direction and were lost in the process of passing through several hands to reach their destination.)[10] Consequently, there was also a system of 'country' or 'area bishops' (*chorepiskopoi*), who were assigned to 'smaller rural settlements in remote areas'.[11] These seem to have had substantial delegated administrative and pastoral responsibilities, but had limited episcopal sacramental functions: the Council of Antioch (341) allowed them to ordain readers, subdeacons, and exorcists; they could only ordain deacons and priests with the express permission of the city bishop.[12] In Cappadocia, they seem to have been appointed from backgrounds more modest than Basil's or Gregory of Nazianzus' landed aristocratic families.[13] A notable number of Basil's letters are addressed to *chorepiskopoi* and their tone does suggest both that he saw them as duty-bound to carry out his instruction as bishop of Caesarea and also that he was heavily dependent on them, Caesarea being the only substantial urban centre in the newly created Cappadocia Prima.[14]

2. Responsibilities and Relationships: the city's soul and the body of Christ.

There were of course, many continuities between being a priest and being a bishop: the administration of the sacraments and preaching, as well as the pastoral care of a particular community (often including local ascetic communities). However, by the fourth century a bishop also had a clearly-

---

9   Basil, *Letter* 198.1, tr. Deferrari, p.101.
10 Basil, *Letter* 198.1, tr. Deferrari, p.99–101.
11 Claudia Rapp, *Holy Bishops in Late Antiquity: The Nature of Christian Leadership in an Age of Transition*, The Transformation of the Classical Heritage 37 (Berkeley: University of California Press, 2005), 173.
12 Aristeides Papadakis, 'Chorepiskopos', in *The Oxford Dictionary of Byzantium*, ed. Alexander P. Kazhdan (Oxford University Press, 2005).
13 Rapp, *Holy Bishops in Late Antiquity*, 178.
14 For their financial role in care of the poor, see Rousseau, *Basil of Caesarea*, 143, 235 n. 6.

established authority over and duty of care for other clergy.[15] This sense of responsibility was heightened for the metropolitan in a province and took up a great deal of his time, to judge from Basil's letters.[16] A brief snap-shot of his vision of episcopal oversight can be found in some letters to his younger fellow-bishop Amphilochius of Iconium.[17] When Basil wrote on the occasion of Amphilochius' consecration as bishop of Iconium (and thus metropolitan of the province of Lycaonia) he advised on his new role: Jesus was sending him not to follow others, but to guide those who are on their way to salvation. Episcopacy should involve the advancing of the gospel (cf. Phil 1:12) and the good ordering of the church. Basil characterises a bishop as a helmsman, a farmer and especially as a steward (*oikonomos*). A steward on a farm is both his master's slave (*doulos*) and has responsibility for his fellow-slaves, for example in administering their food-ration. So, Basil argues, a bishop must serve God and care for his fellow-ministers, perhaps alluding to 1 Peter 4:10 ('Like good stewards (*oikonomoi*) of the manifold grace of God, serve one another with whatever gift each of you has received').[18] He expounds on this theme elsewhere too: for example, good episcopal stewardship is precise, honest and lies best in the hands of just one man who will find other workers for the harvest to labour under him.[19] Similarly, Basil's epistolary eulogy for Musonius, Bishop of Caesarea praises him for being the bulwark, the foundation, the leader, the father of his church – terms which suggest that the weight of responsibility for the church falls on one individual. As Rousseau comments, Basil's praise of Musonius is a picture of a 'man able to relate to his community at every level, playing a variety of roles, and becoming in the end the city's "soul"'.[20]

---

[15] For a brief summary of the bishop's role, see Michael Williams, 'Bishop', in *The Oxford Dictionary of Late Antiquity* (Oxford University Press, 2018) and, in much more detail, Rapp, *Holy Bishops in Late Antiquity* especially chapter 2.

[16] See also Cyprian's letters: Storin and Nicholson, 'Metropolitan'.

[17] The small collection of letters seems to span the period just before Amphilochius' ordination as bishop to shortly before Basil's death from ill-health in 379.

[18] Basil, *Letter* 161.

[19] Basil, Letter 190.

[20] Basil, *Letter* 28 and Rousseau, *Basil of Caesarea*, 155. Many of these roles extended into the secular sphere: Basil was asked to intercede on matters regarding personal patronage, calumny, personal/family property, inheritance disputes, tax immunity, and reduced levies of other kinds: Rousseau, 148, 158–69. Barnim Treucker, 'A Note on Basil's Letters of Recommendation', in *Basil of Caesarea, Christian, Humanist, Ascetic: A Sixteen-Hundredth Anniversary Symposium*, ed. Paul Jonathan Fedwick (Toronto: Pontifical Institute of Mediaeval Studies, 1981), 405–10.

In tension with this, however, is the language Basil uses to express his desire for a more harmonious polity. In one letter, for example, we find him planning a synod of 'men of like mind', 'so that we might govern the churches by the old kind of love, admitting as our own members those of the brethren who come from each part, sending forth as to intimate friends and receiving in turn as from intimates'. He yearns for an age before the divisions of his own time, when men journeyed from one end of the earth to another to meet and when they regarded each other as 'fathers and brothers'.[21] We shall see shortly how Basil attempted to put this kind of vision into practice in institutional terms. On a personal level, Basil's correspondence with Amphilochius testifies to a strong friendship between episcopal colleagues, on which Basil seems to depend greatly. There are matters on which he defers to his friend.[22] He wants Amphilochius to advise him.[23] It brings him relief to share matters of concern with Amphilochius.[24] Ultimately, he and his younger friend share some kind of mutual support in a common task. As Basil writes: 'count me as present with you and as taking part in your good work'.[25] Nevertheless, as we noted at the beginning of this paper, there is always a sense in their correspondence that Basil is the senior bishop, even though technically he has the same status. Furthermore, Basil's friendships were unfortunately fragile: the relationships with Gregory of Nazianzus and Eustathius Bishop of Sebaste which gave him 'assurance and a sense of direction' in his early career foundered (in Gregory's case because of his appointment as Bishop of Sasima; in Eustathius' case on doctrinal grounds).[26] Although one cannot expect all friendships to survive a professional career in controversial times, even a relatively sympathetic modern biographer comments that Basil 'lacked the social diplomacy proper to his task as a bishop'.[27]

The tension between a robust vision of the church as the body of Christ on the one hand and the bishop as the city's soul on the other can be seen especially in the way in which Basil articulates the bishop's duty

---

[21] Basil, Letter 190.
[22] Basil, Letter 190: A bishop from yet another province has written to Basil, assuring him of his loyalty: Basil wants Amphilochius to check his reply over before he sends it back.
[23] Basil, Letter 201.
[24] Basil, Letter 231.
[25] Basil, Letter 202.
[26] For a very nuanced portrait of these and subsequent friendships see Rousseau, *Basil of Caesarea*, chap. 7.
[27] Rousseau, 151.

to speak in and for the church. Good speech was held by Christian authors to be a distinctive feature of the episcopal office. Many of his tasks, administrative, ecclesiastical and political, required the bishop to use his voice, both literally and metaphorically through letters and other writings. For this reason, good bishops were particularly celebrated for their powerful and godly voices – a theme evident in Gregory of Nazianzus' *Oration* 2 on his own ordination, and his memorial orations on his father, on Basil and on Athanasius.[28] Similarly, when Basil consoled the church at Ancyra on the death of their bishop Athanasius, he mourned: 'A mouth has been sealed which abounded in righteous frankness (*parrhesia*) and gushed forth words of grace for building up (*oikodom*) the community (lit. 'brotherhood')'.[29] Christians adapted the classical virtue of frank speech or *parrhesia* to express prophetic boldness inspired by the Spirit. Good episcopal speech was seen as an individual excellence working through grace for the common good – whether that was for building up a congregation or, as we shall see later, for a wider civic community which included the poor. Cappadocian praise of such good speech frequently evokes Pauline language of 'building up and encouragement and consolation', a body with many members or a spiritual house built of many living stones.[30] For example, Basil praises Athanasius for being a pillar and a foundation of his church whose removal destabilised the whole; the limbs of Athanasius' church were knitted together by his leadership.[31]

3. Networks: meetings and episcopal elections.

Despite a series of tense relationships, Basil clearly valued his personal networks and longed for personal interaction. Despite the difficulties of travel, ancient bishops met regularly. As Basil's invitation to Amphilochius in *Letter* 176 indicates, they met for synods (twice yearly provincial synods

---

[28] Gregory of Nazianzus, *Orations* 2, 43, 20, and 21.
[29] Basil, Letter 29 (tr. Deferrari, p.173); cf. on Musonius: 'Silent is his tongue, which like a mighty torrent flooder our ears' (Letter 28, tr. Deferrari, p.165) On Letters 28 and 29 and Basil's developing concept of episcopacy, see Rousseau, *Basil of Caesarea*, 154–55.
[30] E.g. 1 Cor. 14:2–3, 5 and 26. 2 Cor. 10:8-9 and 13:10 (Paul's authority which he associates especially with letter-writing); in deutero-Pauline writings, Eph. 4:12, 16, and 29 ('Let no evil talk come out of your mouths, but only what is useful for building up').
[31] Basil, Letter 29 (tr. Deferrari, p. 173); cf. on Musonius, 'an ornament of the churches, a pillar and foundation of the truth' (Letter 28, tr. Deferrari, p. 161).

had been prescribed by the 5th canon of Nicaea) and for local church festivals or to celebrate the dedication of a new church or shrine. They also met to elect and consecrate a replacement when a bishop died and to settle theological disputes.[32]

The fourth century saw an increase and a formalisation of this kind of episcopal activity. Not only were many of the bishops themselves trained in the skills necessary for this administrative and literary activity (rhetoric being the common grounding for a career in the imperial civil service), the issues to which they were called to apply their skills – administration of people and property and conflict resolution – were similar to those encountered in civil governance.[33] In particular, the continuing trinitarian controversies generated considerable conciliar activity. As Thomas Graumann notes, 'during the fourth century already the production of conciliar documents formed a significant aspect of the bishops' work on the occasion of their meetings, and in addition provided a focal point for much literary activity and epistolary communication between councils'.[34] This work between councils was crucial, because church councils did not meet to weigh up arguments then to vote on them as individuals. Rather, decisions were made by consensus.[35] Consequently, (barring some notable exceptions where tactics close to force were employed) the process of achieving such consensus required sustained collaborative effort in the run-up to the councils themselves. I will discuss some of that theological work below (III.1). Even though there were very clear divisions on theological (and other grounds), from the extant evidence there is a very clear sense of bishops working together for their own chosen cause. The conciliar system was precious to Basil and despite the broken relationships along the way his success in theological argument and creation of pro-Nicene networks was significant, his work eventually bearing fruit after his death in the consensus of bishops at Constantinople in 381.

Alongside conciliar activity, an important way of sustaining pro-Nicene networks was through the promotion of episcopal candidates. The Canons

---

[32]   Thomas Graumann, *The Acts of the Early Church Councils: Production and Character*, Oxford Early Christian Studies (Oxford: Oxford University Press, 2021), 18–19.

[33]   Graumann, *The Acts of the Early Church Councils*, 21.

[34]   Graumann, *The Acts of the Early Church Councils*, 19.

[35]   See Mark S. Smith, *The Idea of Nicaea in the Early Church Councils, AD 431–451*, First edition, Oxford Early Christian Studies (Oxford, United Kingdom: Oxford University Press, 2018), chap. 1 and references, especially to works by Thomas Graumann and Richard Price.

of Nicaea provided that an episcopal candidate needed the consent of the people and his fellow bishops, at least three of whom were required to consecrate. The metropolitan needed to be in agreement.[36] Basil clearly thought that an important part of his job, however, was (in effect) to choose new bishops in his own province – as we have already seen in his appointment of the two Gregories. But he did not stop there. Although bishops were not meant to interfere in appointments outside their own province, Basil probably influenced the appointment and possibly participated in the consecration of Amphilochius (whilst expressing scruples about whether he should 'decline these ordinations beyond our borders').[37] He also advised Amphilochius on appointments in the province of Isauria. Amphilochius may legitimately have had some oversight in this region (which lay to the south of Amphilochius' province of Lycaonia and was notoriously prone to unrest); Basil, however, clearly did not.[38]

Whilst this might seem like an individual overreaching his authority, Basil's motive here was a strategic approach to the defence of Nicene orthodoxy. With a series of emperors who were hostile or at least not supportive of Nicaea, bishops had to work together in its defence. When bishops did intervene in external episcopal appointments it was often in order to promote candidates on one side or other of these debates and they worked in collaborative ways to achieve their aims (as we can see from Basil's correspondence with Amphilochius: this was not Basil acting alone). Given the Nicene canons, the appointment of a pro-Nicene metropolitan or three pro-Nicene bishops could have a profound strategic effect on future appointments in a province. Indeed, Basil's own appointment had been influenced by the involvement of Basil of Samosata, a city which lay (just) over the southern border from Cappadocia. If such practices were not strictly according to Nicaea's canons with regard to episcopal appointments, they were 'bearable anomalies' (to borrow a concept from Mark Chapman's paper in this volume) precisely in the cause of defending the Nicene creed.[39] And in that cause, there was a clear sense of joint endeavour.

---

[36] 4th and 6th Canons of the Council of Nicaea; cf. Williams, 'Bishop'.
[37] Rousseau, *Basil of Caesarea*, 258., citing Basil. *Letters* 138 and 62.
[38] Basil, *Letter* 199 (tr. Deferrari, see p. 71, n. 2) and Rousseau, 260, n.136.
[39] Although, as Andrew Radde-Gallwitz remarks, Basil's appointment 'broke nearly all of [the] rules', Basil's retaining his posts suggests that even his enemies were unable to allege 'serious infringements': Andrew Radde-Gallwitz, *Basil of Caesarea: A Guide to His Life and Doctrine* (Eugene, Or.: Cascade Books, 2012), 92; Rousseau, *Basil of Caesarea*, 147.

III Three examples of episcopal collaboration

A bishop also had other responsibilities besides the exercise of his liturgical duties and the oversight and appointment of other members of the clergy. Some of these responsibilities were financial, such as the administration of church property and bequests, or the disbursement of funds to support widows, orphans and the poor. We will look at Basil's work in this regard below (III.2). First, however, I turn to an example of theological collaboration.

1. The doctrine of the Trinity: opposing Eunomius and his followers

Most people get to know the Cappadocian theologians because of their defence of the doctrine of the Trinity.[40] Historians of doctrine have debated the precise ways in which the three thinkers are dependent on one another and there is a general consensus that while all three firmly defend the co-equality of the three persons of the Trinity, there is a development over time, especially in that Gregory of Nazianzus is far bolder than Basil in declaring that the Spirit is God. But did these writers see themselves as engaged in a collaborative project?

Gregory of Nyssa certainly paints a picture of himself picking up where Basil left off. 'It is right', he writes, 'that we too should do battle with our opponents on this ground where our champion himself led the way in his own book'.[41] While Basil was a mighty general, leading the Lord's army against the Goliath-like Eunomius, Gregory is the small but crafty David

---

[40]   Basil of Caesarea wrote a work *Against Eunomius* in around the year 364, defending 'God's unitary essence and ... the distinctive features that characterize Father, Son and Holy Spirit'. ark DelCogliano and Andrew Radde-Gallwitz, 'Introduction', in *Basil, Against Eunomius* (Washington, D.C.: Catholic University of America Press, 2011), 3. Ten years later he recapitulated some of these themes in his work *On the Holy Spirit*, addressed to Amphilochius of Iconium. Shortly before Basil's death in 378, Eunomius wrote a response, to which Gregory of Nyssa replied in not one but three lengthy works, defending Nicene Christianity together with his older brother Basil's reputation. Gregory of Nazianzus picked up the theological baton in his preaching, especially in his famous *Theological Orations* (Orr. 27-31) preached by invitation in Constantinople in the late summer of 380.

[41]   *Gregory of Nyssa, Against Eunomius,* II.11.14-16. tr. S. G. Hall in Karfíková, Lenka, Scot Douglass, and Johannes Zachhuber, eds. *Gregory of Nyssa, Contra Eunomium II: An English Version with Supporting Studies (Proceedings of the 10th International Colloquium on Gregory of Nyssa, Olomouc, September 15-18, 2004)*. Vigiliae Christianae Supplements 82. (Leiden; Boston: Brill, 2007).

who will finish Goliath off. While one might speculate on what this reveals about their sibling relationship, it is clear that Gregory sees himself as essentially engaged in the same project, albeit after Basil had himself died.[42] The idea of a task to be shared is also evident in two letters which accompanied copies of his work against Eunomius. He sends the first volume to two young men 'as an invitation from us meant to hearten those who are in the full vigour of youth to do battle with our adversaries'.[43] To his brother Peter he sends the first two volumes, not (so he writes) that Peter should join the defence of the faith, but rather so that Peter can advise him as to whether Gregory has undertaken the task appropriately. Gregory was worried that his personal attacks on Eunomius were too vicious – could Peter please advise?[44]

Gregory's words reveal the expectation that it was his job as bishop to defend the faith; he is taking on the role from his former metropolitan and brother Basil; he asks for advice from Peter who, if not yet a bishop, was a respected ascetic leader.[45] Moreover, Gregory sees the production of physical texts as an inherent part of this role. He frets about the obstacles to this production: the availability of copyists, for example, and the fact that he was only lent Eunomius' book for a short while, forcing him to write his own work in a mere seventeen days.[46]

This is just a snap-shot, but it illustrates the way in which bishops like Basil and the two Gregories saw at least part of their episcopal role as the production and circulation of texts which would enable the wider Christian community to defend the Nicene faith. This project was collaborative in the sense that it was a task passed from one to the other, engaged in jointly and consultatively. They relied on colleagues to promote and circulate their work: many works 'against heretics' were in fact addressed and sent to fellow-bishops.[47] They were co-created open-access recipe-books for medicines to protect the church against the disease of heresy. There was

---

[42] Gregory of Nyssa, *Against Eunomius*, II:4–16.
[43] Gregory of Nyssa, *Letter* 15.3.
[44] Gregory of Nyssa, *Letter* 29:3–9.
[45] It is unclear whether Peter was bishop of Sebaste at the time *Letter* 21 was addressed to him (Gregory of Nyssa, *The Letters: Introduction, Translation, and Commentary*, trans. Anna Silvas, Supplements to Vigiliae Christianae 83 (Leiden: Brill, 2007), 206.).
[46] *Letter* 15:2–3; 21:2.
[47] I have developed this idea of collaborative theological literary production in Morwenna Ludlow, *Art, Craft, and Theology in Fourth-Century Christian Authors*, Oxford Early Christian Studies (Oxford: Oxford University Press, 2020), chap. 10.

a broad network of mutual pro-Nicene support – and yet both Gregories lived under Basil's shadow: he was the master and even after he died, there is a sense of several bishops fighting for his inheritance.[48] The hierarchical nature of both episcopal and scholarly authority in the ancient world placed limits on truly equal collaboration.

2. Advocacy and action for the vulnerable

A second task in which the Cappadocians engaged together was preaching. Thematic echoes between certain sermons suggest that they were working over similar ideas together and there is a strong sense of engagement in the same projects. Some sermons, such as Basil and Gregory of Nyssa's homilies on the forty martyrs of Sebaste, were related to local matters (in that case, promoting a local cult).[49] Others, such as their various sermons on the poor, had broader significance. In 368-9, Asia Minor was afflicted by a severe famine. While Basil was still priest in Caesarea, but increasingly while he was the city's bishop, he took practical steps to alleviate the suffering of poor residents. In the short term, Basil persuaded rich merchants to sell their stock-piles of grain so that they could be redistributed. In time, Basil founded an institution on the outskirts of Caesarea which was monastery, hospital, poorhouse and training school for the crafts, all rolled into one.[50] In addition to these practical steps he developed the foundations of a theological response to poverty, which was picked up and developed by the two Gregories. As evidence of this we have a series of sermons which were preached either as a direct response to a famine in or as a result of continuing theological reflection on themes of poverty, disease and exclusion.[51]

As with their doctrinal writings, it is important not to ignore the differences in approach between the three authors: there is not one com-

---

[48] McGuckin, *Saint Gregory of Nazianzus*, chap. 5.

[49] Johan Leemans, 'General introduction', in *'Let us die that we may live': Greek homilies on Christian martyrs from Asia Minor, Palestine and Syria, c. AD 350-c. 450 AD*, ed. Johan. Leemans, Wendy Mayer, Pauline Allen and Boudewijn Dehandschutter (London: Routledge, 2003), 3–47.

[50] see, e. g., Brian Daley, '1998 NAPS Presidential Address Building a New City: The Cappadocian Fathers and the Rhetoric of Philanthropy', *Journal of Early Christian Studies* 7, no. 3 (1 September 1999): 431–61.

[51] Basil's *Homilia in illud: Destruam horrea mea (Hom. 6)*, *Homilia dicta tempore famis et siccitatis (Hom. 8)*, *Homilia in Psalmum 14 (HPs 14)*, Gregory of Nyssa's *De pauperibus amandis (Paup. 1 and 2)*, and Gregory of Nazianzus's *De pauperum amore* or *Peri philopt chias (Or. 14)*.

pletely homogenous 'Cappadocian' theology.[52] Nevertheless, Basil and the two Gregories all worked together on broadly the same project: to argue that human nature is fundamentally one, that everyone without exception is created in the image of God, and that the Christian gospel demanded that the poor, the destitute and lepers be included within the scope of civic philanthropy when, under Roman custom, they were excluded. The bishops exhort their audience, each weaving variations on a distinctive form of Christian rhetoric that forces their audience to notice the bodies of the poor, dwelling on their bodies with an unflinching and uncomfortable gaze. Indeed, one can also argue that the Cappadocians share the same fundamental fault: their close focus on the bodies of the poor draws one's attention to the fact that poor people have no voice. The Cappadocians speak for them, rather than letting their own voices be heard. This is an awkward kind of advocacy, describing the poor from the perspective of the wealthy, aristocratic church insider.[53]

Nevertheless, it is a *shared* approach in which three bishops use their public ecclesial and civic platform to advocate a specific pattern of changed attitudes and shared behaviour. Although much of the impetus came from Basil, their preaching does not spring from a single person's vision but rather from a common theological faith that all people are created in the image of God and that, fundamentally, the goods of the world belong to their divine creator for whom humans are mere stewards. Each bishop builds their preaching in distinctive, but interlinking ways and there is considerable development in the treatment of the themes.

Indeed, the practical philanthropic work can be seen as a collaborative enterprise. It began not with Basil himself, but with another bishop Eustathius of Sebaste who was remarkably effective in recruiting other bishops, especially, but not only Basil, to the cause of a socially-engaged Christianity in the Roman city.[54] His influence on Basil began before Basil was ordained priest, and continued for quite some years before their relationship was ruptured by theological disagreements. In Caesarea, Basil began his philanthropic work while working as priest under the metropolitan Eusebius of Caesarea: although this was a somewhat tense working rela-

---

[52] 'Certainly their "aims" and "lines" were *similar*, but ... in fact each of the three was a pioneer in his own distinctive manner' : Holman, 15.

[53] See especially, Holman, 169.

[54] Rousseau, *Basil of Caesarea*, chap. 7; Susanna Elm, *Virgins of God: The Making of Asceticism in Late Antiquity* (Oxford; New York: Oxford University Press, 1994), passim.

tionship, the continuity between some of Basil's projects before and after his consecration as bishop suggests that Eusebius let this energetic and talented priest have the freedom to develop them. It is clear that the poorhouse in Caesarea was not the only one established by this Christian philanthropic effort and that as bishop Basil greatly relied on his *chorepiscopoi* for the financial and practical administration of projects outside Caesarea. This collaborative project evident in both preaching and action had widespread and long-standing effects.

IV Concluding reflections: the opportunities for and limits to the collaborative exercise of episcope

From the above overview of fourth century episcopacy in Cappadocia, one can see that there were structural and institutional factors which both encouraged and discouraged episcopal cooperation. On the one hand, the role of the metropolitan as first among equals in a province and the use of *chorepiscopoi* meant that there were clear structures in place for collaboration. Canon law (regarding synods and the election of bishops) and custom (regarding the celebration of festivals) worked together to encourage regular meetings. The examples of collaboration we set out in part III illustrate the possibilities of bishops working together on theological and social projects. On the other hand, the underlying concept of 'one city, one bishop' encouraged a certain sense of individual responsibility which is shown with particular clarity in the bishop's role as 'the city's soul'. Furthermore, the very structures underlying the roles of metropolitans and *chorepiscopoi* were profoundly hierarchical, assuming that one individual could expect others to work with (or for) him. Finally, there was the constant practical challenge of travel and communication.

We have seen some of these tensions in Basil's own life. Viewed from one perspective, Basil's vision of episcopacy is of a clear hierarchy: the metropolitan establishing networks through ecclesiastical patronage; the steward working on behalf of his master to manage those under the steward's jurisdiction (albeit as fellow-slaves). Part of the problem is perhaps with our evidence: the natural tendency of the ancient eulogist and the modern biographer alike is to turn their attention to the individual. There is evidence that this somewhat individualist concept of vocation was what contributed to Basil's acute sense of isolation and loneliness in his episcopacy. But this does not mean that he had no sense of collaborative endeavour. Indeed, Basil was acutely, almost neurotically, aware of both the importance and the fragility of the networks which he continuously tried to maintain with fellow-bishops in Anatolia and beyond—and it would be foolish to deny Basil's successes even while acknowledging his failures.[55] Above all, one finds in Basil's correspondence a clear desire for close cooperation with his episcopal colleagues, both on a personal and an institutional level. As a bishop, he yearns for a true meeting of the body of Christ whilst feeling his burdens as the soul of that body.

---

[55] Rousseau's biography is very nuanced in its portrayal of this tension: see especially Rousseau, *Basil of Caesarea*, 148–51, 157–58.

Episcopacy

Historical and theological dignity and personal exercise

Ralf Meister

Dear sisters and brothers, some days ago I traveled to Rome for a visit in the Vatican. At the airport I met a descendant of the British royal family, Ernst August Jr. He stems from the House of the Guelphs. As many people will be aware, the ties between the Kingdom of Hanover and the British Crown lasted for about 120 years, beginning in 1714 with the accession of George I, Elector of Hanover as King of the United Kingdom. Ernst August Jr. lives in Hanover and I have got to know him through many receptions. There we stood face to face, casually dressed for traveling, and I greeted him with the words: 'Your Royal Highness'. He replied: 'Most Honorable [Hochwürden]', and both of us had to laugh.

What is meant by 'Most Honourable'? A year ago, I was elected by a chapter of lay persons as the protestant abbot of a monastery. This monastery is a Cistercian monastery. It is situated 30 kilometres northwest of Hanover in the small town of Loccum. It was founded in 1163 when Count Wulbrand of Hallermund donated it to the Cistercians. This means that right up to the present day we still adopt the Cistercian motto: *'Porta Patet; Cor Magis'* [The gate is open, the heart even more]. Everybody is very welcome to pay us a visit! Over the centuries land was added to the monastery, and a number of crises were overcome. The monastery survived the Reformation because in September 1530 the Abbot of Loccum appeared before the Diet of Augsburg when he asked Charles V to transform the monastery into a free imperial foundation. This was enacted. The monks followed the ideas of the reformation throughout the sixteenth century and soon made the monastery Lutheran. But the monks did not leave the monastery: they continued to worship and the daily offices but in a manner which followed the reformation. They opened the church to the local congregation and engaged in pastoral care. Nevertheless, the feeling of a certain affiliation with the Cistercian order lasted through the centuries and still exists. Just before writing this paper I visited the General Abbot of the Cistercians Mauro-Giuseppe Lepori in Rome.

During the seventeenth century Lutheran pastors were accommodated in the convent in place of the monks, and the house was opened for '*Hospites*', that is, future pastors who were waiting for a position and who were consequently able to prepare for their future ministry. This developed into the Theological Seminary which has been functioning in the monastery for over 200 years. It is one of the oldest seminaries in Germany and the monastery is considered to be one of the best-preserved Cistercian monasteries.

As abbot I also preside over the supervising committee of the biggest insurance company in Lower Saxony, the VGH. The reason for this is that one of my predecessors, Abbot Ebell of Loccum, 250 years ago pioneered the idea of fire insurance. The abbot in Loccum occupied a particular position of spiritual authority in the Kingdom of Hanover even before there was a bishop. When the head of the Board of Directors of the VGH addressed me during my institution ceremony, he called me 'Most Honourable', even though the title 'most Honourable' has long disappeared from colloquial German. In earlier times it was used in the life of the church to address persons in higher leading ministries, including bishops and abbots, although nowadays such a tile is no longer in use. The point of this illustration is to show the importance of the title 'Most Honourable' in the identity of the VGH, whose foundation goes back to the ideas of a clergyman. People at the reception including younger employees used this honorary title to address me. It was a title that reflected the foundation narrative. In this it is similar to the authority of the abbot, which comes from a time that is long since passed. This points to a strange world which continues to shine into our largely secular society.

It is not only with reference to the VGH, however, where seemingly outmoded titles continue to be used. It is also true of the wider secular society. This includes the title of 'Bishop'. This particular form of ecclesiastical ministry points back to the foundation stories of our society, whose origins were deeply shaped by religion. The title 'Bishop' represents a socio-cultural DNA that persists until today, in much the same way as in old church buildings and cathedrals. It is unlikely that many people would be able to give a detailed description of the precise qualities and duties of an abbot or a bishop. But the notion that this old-fashioned title describes an authority that stands for basic ethical orientation, piety and charity would probably be shared by most of them. The bishop is perceived as speaking for the truth, even when people do not necessarily share it. This is why the scandals concerning to the behaviour of bishops in relation to sexual abuse inflict a massive loss of credibility on the church as a whole. In the VGH company 'Most Honourable' stands for a spiritual orientation which is not considered a liability to the company, but an asset. It says something like this: 'We stand for values.' This, in turn, is important for marketing.

I have also experienced this ambivalence in my ministry as a bishop in a slightly different way. During the initial phase of my tenure I tried, perhaps out of a position of insecurity, to be as popular and approachable as possible. I invited many people who asked how to address me just to use my family name and not the title 'Herr *Landesbischof*'. (There is an irony because my name 'Meister' means 'master', so I often said: 'Just call me Master', as the people used to call Jesus – as in Luke 17:13, and Matthew 23:36 where the Luther Bible 1984 translates the Greek: '*Meister, welches ist das höchste Gebot im Gesetz?*' ['Master, which is the highest commandment?']) I realized that this invitation disappointed the people. They would have liked to use the title 'bishop'. And when people came to me with a problem, I often tried during the conversation to throw light on different sides of the problem and to propose directions of travel and points for discussion. But often I sensed the expectation was different. People wanted the bishop to take a decision. They seemed to want an answer to the question: What does the bishop say? The bishop describes the position of the church. As Andreas Reckwitz put it in a sociological study, in a 'society of singularities', there is an expectation towards bishops and other 'Most Honourables' to describe order and unity.[1] The role was not to describe what is complex, but to outline what is clear and binding.

This attitude is not only encouraged by contemporary sociological and psychosocial dynamics, but also by the tradition. The ministries of the church are old – extremely old. Even to individuals who have few ties to the history of Christianity, the ministries have an origin which is an integral part of our culture. This force helps to keep the importance of the bishop's ministry alive till this present day. Its historical profile adds to its authority within the church and provides it with a – sometimes ambivalent – prestige and a particular public function. This importance is reinforced by the media. Bishops are expected to make public statements. The bishop's ministry represents the top of the institution – even in a liberal

---

[1]   Andreas Reckwitz, *Die Gesellschaft der Singularitäten: Zum Strukturwandel der Moderne* (Berlin: Suhrkamp, 2019).

democracy. Even if within the protestant churches the hierarchy of ministries was supposed to have been abolished, it still persists in the public opinion. In principle, according to Martin Luther, we are all bishops. He writes: 'For whatever issues from baptism, may boast that it has been consecrated priest, bishop, and Pope.'[2] Such an explanation is very difficult to communicate, although equality before God and participation play a role. Outside the church these images do not represent the vision of the bishop. Public opinion thinks hierarchically, including within the protestant church. This is reinforced by the canonical authority of the bishop in the Roman-Catholic Church. And this authority is often projected onto the protestant churches, sometimes to good effect, and sometimes bad.

This public attention which is paid to the ministry of the bishop leads us again and again in our theological and ecclesiological discussions to a self-critical examination of our own history and of the development of our ministries. We had already begun to look at various historical examples of the formation and characterization of the church's ministries at the last Theological Conference, particularly the office of the bishop and the ways in which episcopacy is exercised within our churches. History is a wide field. It provides sufficient material to interpret the development of hierarchy and the position of the bishop's ministry in the churches in one way or another. There is no consistent and unanimous interpretation of episcopacy, just as there is no continuous history without changes, ruptures and adjustments. Our history, including church history, remains fragmentary and opens up to the most variable interpretations. Adelmann von Lüttich (Liège), Bishop of Brescia in Northern Italy in the eleventh century, wrote: 'Everything has been settled in an excellent way, nothing new can be created anymore. Yes, God hates the innovators.' Unfortunately, it seems to me, this idea of 'unchangeability' characterises many of our parishes just as much as it does at the level of church leadership. This is especially true of our Roman Catholic brothers and sisters. Such phrases reveal a particular understanding of the church: that the church proclaims eternal truths which do not need to be renewed or modernized.

The discussion of the extent to which faith needs further development and to undergo changes has accompanied Christianity for 2000 years. It starts with the Council of the Apostles in Acts 15, and continues through all the Councils. That said, not all church doctrines are the same. The most binding form of church doctrine is represented by dogmas. For the

---

[2] *Schriften 1519/20* (einschl. Predigten, Disputationen), WA 6, 408, 11f.

hermeneutics of doctrines, it is crucial to realize that many dogmas developed as a means to arbitrate and to resolve conflicts. In the first centuries of church history councils often defined dogmas in times of crisis, especially when conflicts threatened to divide the church. Dogmas are meant to end a conflict through a binding doctrine, reduce complexity and limit diversity. Among such dogmas are the definition of the Holy Trinity, the essence of Christ as true God and true Man, and the fixing of the canon. The definition of episcopacy is not part of this within the early church because church teachers – just to mention Hippolytus – offered an interpretation of the scriptures concerning this question. In his 'Apostolic Tradition' composed around the year 200, the spiritual leader of a local urban congregation and its worship was counted as a bishop, chosen by this congregation and consecrated by the bishops of neighbouring congregations. But on different levels the doctrine of the church has changed over the centuries to quite different degrees. The tension between continuity and discontinuity has stimulated the vital development of dogmas and of church doctrine from the very beginning. All changes were supposed to be so well tied in with the tradition that they would not destroy the continuity of the history of one's own church. Even the Reformation fits in with this pattern because the Reformers did not want to establish a new church. They saw themselves as reformers within the old church. Often ruptures from the tradition are not declared to be such. There is a particular method for this process: it is claimed that the new doctrine goes back to an earlier 'purer' state of affairs. According to the church historian John O'Malley, Roman Catholic priest and Jesuit, this method is called 'ressourcement'.[3] It is a category alongside 'aggiornamento' to understand adaptations of dogmas or convictions as continuity within discontinuity. This applies even when they bring with them massive changes.

Again and again we see how our interpretations of issues of church history are subject to our various theological presuppositions and wishes. This leads to various questions: which phase or which events in history are we choosing? Which documents are we including in our research, and in what order of importance are we ranking them? What set of practices are we relying on? Which facets in the history of ideas and in cultural history are we taking seriously, and which ones are we neglecting? Together we are looking for an interpretation of the discontinuities within the his-

---

[3]   See, for instance, John O'Malley, *What Happened at Vatican II?* (Cambridge, Mass: Harvard University Press, 2010).

torical development of episcopacy in our churches which can bring us to-gether, which will bring us together into a perfect communion. We know that there is no consistent historical evidence for this aspiration which will satisfy everyone. Despite all the scientific insights and the application of reason to the subject the day will probably come when, to speak with Kierkegaard, it is time to jump!

The churches which came out of Reformation brought deep disconti-nuities into the history of ecumenical Christianity across the world. This also proved the case with the ministry of the bishop. Such discontinuities, I would suggest, are not primarily separating, but ways that open up some-thing new. *The* Church does not exist except in the form of *particular* churches. The Church is not an entity alongside or in addition to the par-ticular churches, but it is the one body of Christ in which all Christians partake within their respective churches. Being a member of a church means being a member of the body of Christ. In this sense the church is the communion of believers, the *congregatio sanctorum*. In order to live as a member of the body of Christ, one has to participate in what makes a church a church: the proclamation of the Gospel in Word and Sacrament and the conviction that God works through that faith in our daily lives. This is the journey we share. We walk together in the fragments of our own confessional histories as the one people of God, towards a fully visible unity, even in the here and now.

Discontinuities

Let me briefly describe the principal discontinuity of my church as a church of the Reformation. What may not be evident to everyone is that the first 'discontinuity-in-continuity' is the Reformation itself. But in its central goals the Reformation was a 'ressourcement'. Martin Luther had no agenda of his own for the implementation of the reformation and for the estab-lishment of a new institutional protestant church. He himself never in-tended to create a new church, but to transform the old one. Many dog-matic, liturgical, theological and legal questions were re-ordered. At the same time, a new understanding of the exercise of the ministry of the bishop developed. It came about through the return of the reformers and the humanists to the Holy Scriptures. The confession of the Lutheran churches, the Augsburg Confession (*Confessio Augustana*), expressed the desire to recognize and to continue the episcopate in the form that it had been passed on from the early church and as it had been practised in the church. Reformation never called for the abolition of the historic episcopate, seeking only its comprehensive reform. There are many theories as to why it was important to maintain the episcopate during the Reformation. It is hard to assess which are the most important. The Augsburg Confession was a text written for political mediation. So, we might ask, was it the political circumstances or pastoral pragmatism or theological wisdom that stood behind the maintenance of the episcopate? It is highly likely that the structure of the church's ministry was not questioned at all at that time. What was criticized was the ways in which hierarchical authority had developed and was practised. Episcopal authority had to stand before the bar of the Gospel.

The Reformation did not fight against the episcopate, but for the Gospel. And this Gospel was obscured by the work of the bishops during the Middle Ages. During the Reformation, however, the question of 'apostolic succession' hardly played a role. Although it is true that the practice of ordination in the Latin churches in the Middle Ages maintained continuity with the order of the early church, this was for purely canonical and not explicitly theological reasons. Apostolic succession was not a controversial topic in the first decades of the sixteenth century. Right up till the Diet of Wittenberg in 1541 the Reformers neither confirmed nor repudiated the concept, and seemed to have as little interest in it as their contemporaries. Although Luther criticized the pretence of power of the episcopacy and repudiated the idea of consecration, just as he did with the papacy, he upheld the office as such. For Luther there is no difference in principle between a bishop and a pastor. The ministry of preaching is 'the highest ministry in Christianity'.[4] In his essay 'Example: how to consecrate a Christian bishop' Luther similarly describes the duties of a bishop to be like those of a pastor: 'namely that a bishop shall be holy, preach, baptize, forgive and retain sins, comfort souls and help them to eternal life'.[5] For Luther, 'bishop' and 'pastor' are synonyms: their sole duty is to serve the congregations with the proclamation of the Word and the administration of the sacraments.

It was only in their responsibility for other congregations, inasmuch as they cared for pastors in the congregations, that there were specific duties to fulfil. In his address of 1520, 'To the Christian Nobility of the Ger-

---

[4] *Predigten und Schriften 1523*, WA 11, 415, 30ff.
[5] *Exempel, einen rechten christlichen Bischof zu weihen.* Geschehen zu Naumburg Anno 1542, 20. Januar, WA 53, 253, 6ff.

man Nation'[6] Luther elaborated this criticism at length for the first time when he asked who bore the blame for the situation of the church in the Middle Ages. His answer was clear: the bishops and the Pope! It was they, according to Martin Luther, who bore responsibility for the desperate condition of the church. In turn, he asked as to who could remedy the situation. His answer was again clear: the nobility, the worldly authorities. Even if little of the circumstances of the beginning of the sixteenth century can be transferred to our times, Martin Luther's pointed criticism of the episcopacy is a live issue once again; indeed, it has gained a new importance. Protestant churches continually had difficulties in coming to terms with the office of the bishop. Today a number of senior clergy in the fold of the EKD-churches are called 'church president' or *Präses*, but they are nothing other than bishops. Their duties in dealing with congregations, church districts, bureaucracy, and synods are similar.

So, are the clergy a sign of weakness in the churches? Are there people in leading offices in the church able to deal with the tasks and many expectations placed on the clergy for integrity, care for youth, spiritual formation? Is the concentration on spiritual tasks sufficient to prevent them from being overwhelmed by administrative duties? Luther criticizes the bishops of his time with harsh words, while holding the episcopate in high esteem: 'bishops, priests, and above all the doctors of the universities, who are paid for this, have written and shouted against this unanimously as it was their duty.'[7] They were supposed to counteract the spiritual decay of the church. In this duty, however, they failed. Is the bishop's office open to fundamental reform? Was it ever able to be so? They probably never stood for reform; their primary role was and still is to establish and conserve the church. Or is it not an urgent task for the church to be lived, thought and shaped more consistently 'from below', both during the Coronavirus crisis and in times of sexual abuse scandals and the painful process that follows? 'Therefore, the consecration of a bishop is as if instead of the whole congregation he took one of the crowd, who all have the same power.'[8]

Luther's attitude fundamentally changed when the catholic bishops in Germany refused to implement the Reformation and did not even allow protestant preaching. This compelled demands for a new order within the church. It also led to a clarification of the question of the leading ministerial

---

[6]   WA 6, 381–475.
[7]   WA 6, 426, 21f.
[8]   WA 6, 407, 29f.

office. That was not only a question to be solved within the church, but it became a question of church and state. The legal system of the Church and Empire became partly obsolete. Since the time of Otto the Great the integration of the Church into the Empire had been a characteristic trait of the *Corpus Christianum* in Germany. This close connection of Church and State deprived the church of a constitution of its own, structures of its own, as well as a synod and a primate of its own. When the bishops gathered they met as imperial princes during the diets. This meant that Reformation was not just an event within the church, but was political from the beginning. As a consequence, this led to the fact that Luther called on the political rulers to exercise oversight. This brought into being new forms of church order and in a certain way a clarification of the leading spiritual ministry. The lack of clarity which became evident in the beginning of the 1520s – in parishes, monasteries, charities, as well as during the Peasants' War – led Luther to seek a new order for the church. When the Diet of Speyer decided in 1526 that the edict of Worms should be applied in ways that could be justified before God and the Emperor, this meant that the reformation was in the hands of the princes and the free cities.

In consequence, a much higher responsibility was devolved upon princes than before. Until 1520 Luther had only called upon the princes for help in relation to certain grievances; after that year far more extensive powers were required. Visitations would be conducted by the princes, and they would install pastors. Luther called the princes 'emergency bishops'. From then on, the princes of the protestant lands would not only establish a new church order but also use their office and authority to stand up for the Gospel against the Emperor, the Empire and the Pope. This meant that the Augsburg Confessions was signed not only by protestant theologians, but also by many princes, who presented it to the Emperor. Of course, in the view of Luther and Melanchthon, the princes were to take over only the external government in the church, rather than determining the doctrine or exercising church discipline. Even though the consistories established by the state churches were under the authority of the princes, they were able to preserve a certain degree of independence for the church.

So, it can be said that the former power of the bishops in the protestant territories was divided until 1919 with the abolition of the church government by the princes. From the Reformation the personal spiritual duties of bishops such as preaching, administration of the sacraments, and ordination were transferred to pastors, superintendents or consistories. Other aspects were taken over by the 'emergency bishops' which meant all temporal aspects were placed exclusively under the jurisdiction of the prince. This meant that the position of the princes became more and more powerful. As early as the end of the 16th century it was assumed that the power of supervision and jurisdiction as well as the placement of personnel and the church legislation was the privilege of the princes.

The loss of the episcopate led to the establishment of a position of oversight within the church, termed 'superintendent'. This term was simply a translation of *episkopos* into Latin, which had been used earlier by Jerome and Augustine. These superintendents became the first permanent office of the protestant church order, developing out of the process of visitation. On a regional level they were also called *Generalsuperintendent* or, as in the Church of Hanover, *Landessuperintendent*. Although originally the title was initially rather provisional, superintendents would last a long time in Germany. Even today they still exist in many churches as leaders of church districts. Here Germany differs from other Lutheran countries such Denmark where the historical title for the church's supervising ministry of bishop was resumed as early as the 17th century. Before 1920, any use of the term 'bishop' was dependent on its legal relationship to the political authorities. In short, one can say that the continuation of the historical episcopate was impossible not only for theological, but also for political reasons. The ties between the Empire and the episcopate made it impossible to continue with this relationship, because protestant bishops were legally excluded by the imperial constitution. The Religious Peace of Augsburg of 1555 protected the spiritual princes who personally accepted the Augsburg Confession without punishment or loss of civil rights, but at the same time they were deprived of their church offices, sinecures, imperial revenues and temporal authority. During the expansion of Reformation in the War of Schmalkalden in 1546/1547 the Elector of Saxony and the Landgrave of Hesse paid for their adherence to the Reformation with the loss of their power and many years in prison.

This history of discontinuities through the centuries in many ways is focused on the institution of episcopacy, with the bishop's vocation and ordination, as well as his or her position in the ordering of the church. It is impossible to understand protestant church history and the important but also unique role of episcopacy within the EKD without having a grasp of the numerous and multi-faceted developments of the first half of the 16th century. This discontinuity continues through the discussion over the introduction of the office of bishop in the protestant churches in the 20th century. And the office of bishop was subject to fundamental reappraisal during the time of National Socialism. At the same time, they reflect the peculiar German relationship between the church and the state, and which was put in order after the dissolution of political episcopacy in the various federal states through state-church agreements. Right up till the present day there are regional churches in Germany whose borders are coterminous with those of the former princely territories.

Melanchthon commented on the brief moment in which opportunities arose to return to a historical succession in the religious conversations before the diet of Regensburg. Writing in 1539 in 'On the Church and the Authority of the Word of God', he countered those who 'claim that the church is the state of the bishops and who tie it to the orderly succession of bishops, just as empires have their stability through the succession of princes. But in the church it is otherwise. It is a union that is not tied to the succession of bishops, but to the Word of God.'[9] So it remains an irony of history that the succession of princes as emergency bishops retained a direct influence on the church, sometimes for centuries.

Conclusion

There is an anecdote that has been told about a visit of Justin Welby to Pope Francis. Before starting their proper ecumenical conversation, the Archbishop of Canterbury asked: 'What is the difference between a liturgist and a terrorist?' The answer was this: 'You can reason with a terrorist.' Photographs are said to show the two in loud laughter. Let us replace the liturgist with a dogmatist. Is it possible to reason with a dogmatist? Is he capable of reassessing a situation so that it can be interpreted in such a way as to allow for a common approach towards a peaceful, spiritual communion? The Meissen Commission has pursued exactly this vision. It insists that further understanding will result in further convergence. This is its goal: convergence through a differentiated consensus in which we respect the otherness of the other, just as we do when we look at the different ways of life in our own congregations. We are seeking what we have in common. And we transform that into a bridge over which we can walk together. 'The quality of ecumenical texts cannot be measured by the extent and the profundity of the consensus formulated in them, but by the fact that as texts they *can be coherently understood and interpreted within*

---

[9]   Robert Stupperich, *Melanchthons Werke in Auswahl* 1 (Gütersloh: C. Bertelsmann, 1951), 330.

the mental framework of the participating partner churches. They may not be one-dimensional, but they have to embrace a number of different codes that means that they can be adapted to the highly complex mental worlds ... of the two churches in such a way that both of them see them as a consistent extrapolation of their plausibility structures. That is ... truly an art'.[10]" That was written by Ingolf Dalferth ten years after the Meissen-Declaration. This high art we pursue, unflinchingly, faithfully, and with courage. And many elements of the years of our common work have shown how closely we are already connected and how we are serving the goal of unity.

During my visit to Rome I received a small booklet from the president of the Pontifical Council for Promoting Christian Unity Kurt Cardinal Koch, with the title: *The Bishop and Christian Unity: An Ecumenical Vademe-cum*.[11] To be honest, this does not help us in the sensitive topic of apostolicity and episcopacy, because it is addressed to the Roman Catholic bishops alone. But it is worth sharing some sentences from it which relate to the ecumenical movement: 'The Dialogue of Love deals with encounter at the level of everyday contacts and co-operation, nurturing and deepening the relationship we already share through baptism. The Dialogue of Truth concerns the vital doctrinal aspect of healing division among Christians. The Dialogue of Life includes the opportunities for encounter and collaboration with other Christians in pastoral care, in mission to the world and through culture' (§15). This is a good description of the road along which we have travelled as the Meissen Commission into our fourth decade: A Dialogue of Love, a Dialogue of Truth and a Dialogue of Life. We will continue to travel further along it together.

---

[10]   Ingolf Dalferth, *Auf dem Weg der Ökumene. Die Gemeinschaft evangelischer und anglikanischer Kirchen nach der Meissener Erklärung* (Leipzig: EVA, 2002), 250.

[11]   4 December 2020 at: https://press.vatican.va/content/salastampa/en/bollet-tino/pubblico/2020/12/04/201205a.html (accessed 19 March 2022).

What did a bishop think he was doing?

Episcopal oversight in practice in England's age of reform (c. 1830–1850)

Frances Knight

Introduction

This paper builds on Mark Chapman's article, 'The Politics of Episcopacy' which was originally written for the Meissen conference in 1999.[1] It provides a further interrogation of the novelty of the Anglo-Catholic emphasis on the idea of apostolic succession in the episcopal ministry as providing a basis for authority in the Church, an idea famously set out by John Henry Newman in the first of the *Tracts for the Times* in 1833. I shall do this by means of a brief summary of some salient points from Peter Nockles' influential 1994 study *The Oxford Movement in Context* in which he analyses the roots of the apostolic paradigm, and follow that with a case study of Bishop John Kaye (1793–1853), bishop of Lincoln from 1827–53. Kaye was a bishop throughout the Oxford Movement era, and reacted publicly to its pronouncements mainly through his episcopal charges, which he delivered to the clergy of his diocese at three yearly intervals. I will then consider some of the practical ways in which he exercised oversight in his vast diocese – at the time the largest in the Church of England – in order to try to answer the question what did he think he was doing, and how did he do it?

Kaye is an appropriate subject for more detailed investigation, not least because he was regarded as one of the most learned churchmen of his day. A bishop first of Bristol from 1820 to 1827, and then Lincoln, from 1827 to 1853, he had plenty of time to consider the manner in

---

[1] Mark D. Chapman, 'The Politics of Episcopacy' *Anglican and Episcopal History* 69:4 (December 2000): 474–503. Also in in Ingolf U. Dalferth and Paul Oppenheim (eds), *Einheit bezeugen / Witnessing to Unity: Ten Years after the Meissen Declaration* (Frankfurt am Main: Lembeck, 2004), 150–69.

which he was exercising oversight. As Regius Professor of Divinity from 1816 to 1827, he had pioneered the study of patristics at Cambridge, and we may assume that he was familiar with the ideas about episcopal authority that had been laid out by Archbishop James Ussher, when he had considered the Ignatian letters. It appeared that Ignatius (c. 35 – c. 107) had provided extremely early evidence of the role of bishops in his twelve surviving letters, but there had long been an issue over whether these letters were authentic, or forgeries. Ussher solved the problem by demonstrating the authenticity of some of the letters, and also argued that there was evidence for bishops and clergy operating in a spirit of close cooperation at this early date.[2] Kaye's view of episcopacy seems to have been partly informed by Ussher's perspective. He was one of the five bishops who were the original members of the Ecclesiastical Commission, and he saw himself, and was seen by others, as being a very authoritative voice in the Church of England. Kaye was a high churchman of conservative temperament, and his thinking was inevitably shaped by the age in which he was living. But listening to him again does give us access into a large vista of the mid-nineteenth century Church of England, and to that constituency that read Newman's Tract 1 and found the idea that bishops were 'Representatives of the Apostles, and Angels of the Churches' alien and unconvincing. Although, as Mark Chapman and others have shown, it was Newman's ideas, further solidified by Charles Gore, that would prove particularly influential in shaping later ideas about the Anglican episcopate, it is important to appreciate that it could well have turned out differently, and that there were other influential mid-nineteenth century voices, and other visions of episcopal oversight.

Pre-Tractarian high church views of apostolic succession

The variety of Anglican views within the existing high church constituency in the immediate pre-Tractarian period is a central argument within Peter Nockles' landmark study *The Oxford Movement in Context: Anglican High Churchmanship, 1760–1857* (1994), and in his subsequent publications.[3] He makes the point that 'it suited the purposes of Tractarian rhetoric

---

[2]   See Alan Ford, *James Ussher: Theology, History and Politics in Early-Modern Ireland and England* (Oxford: Oxford University Press 2007), 223–256.

[3]   For a recent appraisal and appreciation of Nockles' contribution to our understanding of high churchmanship, among other topics, see William Gibson and Geordan

to portray their advocacy of apostolical succession as the recovery of an ancient truth lost sight of in the "deadness" of eighteenth-century Anglicanism'.[4] In fact, and unsurprisingly to anyone who knows anything about the history of the Church of England, there were diverse views, even among high church Anglican clergy who might have appeared outwardly of similar mind on ecclesiological issues. There were some, including the future prime minister and Anglo-Catholic W. E. Gladstone, and the influential Bishop C. J. Blomfield of London, who regarded the Tractarian teaching on apostolic succession as novel. It was something that they thought had not surfaced since the time of the non-juror William Law over one hundred years earlier. But there were others, including the high church wine merchant Joshua Watson, who asserted, somewhat vaguely, that those who believed the doctrine could be numbered in the thousands. This seems grossly exaggerated, and Nockles, who is admired for his thoroughness in these matters, provides evidence of only ten clerical authors in the period from 1770–1820 who expressed support for this version of the apostolic paradigm. One was John Oxlee, who in 1820 provided 'a continued and uninterrupted list of Christian bishops from the Blessed Apostles Peter, Paul and John, down to the present prelates of Canterbury, York and London.'[5]

Kaye seems to have had little sympathy for this kind of episcopal genealogy, which to any serious student of church history was likely to stretch credibility beyond the bounds of possibility. In his book on Tertullian, he noted that Tertullian had tried to confound the heretics with just this kind of thing, but then rapidly moved on to criticise him for being apparently unable to distinguish adequately between bishops and presbyters.[6] The conclusion he wished to draw was that Tertullian believed that the Apostolic Churches were independent of each other but equal in rank and authority.[7] It seemed that Kaye was trying to find an ancient precedent for the branch theory, that Roman, Orthodox and Anglican Churches were branches of the Catholic Church, the Anglicans a pure branch, and the

Hammond (eds.,) *Religion in Britain, 1660–1900: Essays in Honour of Peter B. Nockles. Bulletin of the John Rylands Library* 97:1 (Spring, 2021).

4   Peter B. Nockles, *The Oxford Movement in Context: Anglican High Churchmanship 1760–1857* (Cambridge: Cambridge University Press 1994), 146.

5   Nockles, *Oxford Movement*, 148–9.

6   John Kaye, *The Ecclesiastical of the Second and Third Centuries, Illustrated from the Writings of Tertullian* (Cambridge, 1826), 233–4.

7   Kaye, *Tertullian*, 236.

other two corrupted.[8] If so, this would align with the standard contemporary high church belief that the Fathers had really been Anglicans without knowing it. For example, Kaye had no difficulty in suggesting that Tertullian's doctrinal position was the pre-cursor of the 39 Articles, an opinion enthusiastically endorsed by a reviewer.[9]

Bishop Kaye's response to Tractarian claims

How did Bishop Kaye react to Tractarian attempts to reframe the Church of England in a way that magnified the authority of bishops? He was of the same mind as his close friend and episcopal colleague Charles Blomfield: the Tractarian version of apostolic succession was not a doctrine he recognised. In common with most of his brother bishops, his initial response to the Oxford Movement Tracts had been cautiously positive.[10] In his charge of 1838, he referred to the Tractarians as 'a society of learned and pious men connected with the University of Oxford, whose object is to recal [sic] the minds of men to the contemplation of primitive Christianity', although he qualified this by suggesting that they were influenced by 'too indiscriminate an admiration of antiquity, and of endeavouring to revive practices and modes of expression which the Reformers wisely relinquished.'[11] This was revealing, in view of the fact that Kaye remained active as a patristics scholar for the whole of his life, and so had had plenty of opportunity to contemplate the strengths and weaknesses of the early

---

[8]   Kaye returned to this idea in his final Charge of 1852. 'The ground on which we must take our stand [against the setting up of the Roman Catholic hierarchy in England and Wales] is that our Church is a branch of the Catholic Church; and that the Church of Rome, though it calls itself exclusively the Church, is no more than a branch – an erring branch. In the primitive times all the Churches of Christendom – the Churches of Jerusalem, of Antioch, of Ephesus, of Corinth, of Rome, were equal and independent; and the unity of the Catholic Church was maintained by the communion of members with each other; not by the domination of one member over the rest' (John Kaye, *Nine Charges Delivered to the Clergy of the Diocese of Lincoln, with some other works* (London, 1854), 444–5). For more on the branch theory, see Nockles, *Oxford Movement in Context*, 153. The leaders of the Oxford Movement eventually gave up the theory.

[9]   See 'Bishop of Bristol's Ecclesiastical History', *Quarterly Theological Review* IV (June 1826): 33–48, esp. 42–43.

[10]   The same pattern of changing reactions to the Tractarians is found in the charges of Bishops Phillpotts, Denison, Monk, Bagot, Bethell and Blomfield.

[11]   Kaye, *Nine Charges*, 145–6.

Christian world.[12] By the early 1840s, Kaye was becoming horrified by Newman's readiness to remould and potentially sacrifice the Church of England's historic formularies (the Thirty-nine Articles) in pursuit of his own preconceived notion of what was primitive. He also had to cope with the early conversion to Rome of one of his diocesan clergy, Bernard Smith of Leadenham, in 1841, and the large amount of hostile press coverage of what was then seen as a major scandal.[13] Newman's own conversion in 1845 merely confirmed what was becoming a prevalent view that Newman had been destabilising the Church from within, promoting ideas, such as apostolic succession, which are not implied in the Thirty-nine Articles, or indeed in the Book of Common Prayer ordination service.

Kaye responded with a lengthy attempt to explain and defend the English Reformation as the birthplace of Anglicanism, and to press for continued assent to what he termed the 'natural' meaning of the Articles, and for the exclusive use of the Book of Common Prayer, the twin supports which had maintained the Church of England for centuries.[14] His charge of 1846 amounted to a bitter attack on the Tractarians. But in his later charges he turned to other matters, which is unsurprising in view of the fact that virtually none of the clergy in the almost 1,300 parishes in his diocese showed support for Tractarianism during his lifetime.[15] This raises the question 'why so few?' Part of answer may be found in the smaller

---

[12] He published on Tertullian and the ecclesiastical history of the second and third centuries in 1826, Justin Martyr (*Some account of the writings and opinions of Justin Martyr* (London: Rivington, 1829), Clement of Alexandria (*Some account of the writings and opinions of Clement of Alexandria*, (London: Rivington, 1835)) and Athanasius and the Council of Nicaea (*Some account of the Council of Nicea, in connexion with the life of Athanasius* (London: Rivington, 1853). These works were highly regarded in their day, and Justin Martyr was still in print in 1917.

[13] R. W. Ambler, 'The Conversion to Roman Catholicism of Bernard Smith of Leadenham, 1842', *Lincolnshire History and Archaeology* xiv (1979): 57–61.

[14] Kaye, *Nine Charges*, 299.

[15] The number of parishes within the diocese fluctuated as various archdeaconries were added and subtracted as the ecclesiastical reform process got underway. The number was 1273 in 1833, when the diocese was at its largest. A significant amount of Kaye's Lincolnshire correspondence was edited by Rod Ambler, and it is striking how little of it was concerned with Tractarianism. See R.W. Ambler, (ed.), *Lincolnshire Correspondence of John Kaye, Bishop of Lincoln, 1827–53*, Lincoln Record Society 94 (Woodbridge: Boydell Press, 2006). I reached the same conclusion when researching my own PhD thesis, Frances M. R. Knight, 'Bishop, Clergy and People: John Kaye and the Diocese of Lincoln, 1827–53', University of Cambridge PhD, 1990.

number of Oxford graduates in his diocese, compared to those from Cambridge. But it also seems likely that many of the young men who had sat at Newman's feet in Oxford either abandoned, or kept very quiet about, their newly minted Oxford theology when they found themselves faced with the realities of parochial life in the East Midlands.

How did Kaye express episcopal oversight?

When Kaye mentions bishops at all, it is often in the form of condemnation of what he termed 'the extravagant pretensions of the Roman pontiff', which in the mid-1840s was coupled with an anxiety about the possibility that England might indeed move further into the Roman orbit.[16] There was an urgent need to articulate an alternative vision of the episcopal role. Kaye believed that the authority of bishops was derived from society's official recognition and sanction of their suitability. In his own case, this was recognition of his significant academic achievements, and the recognition, formally conferred by the crown, and mediated by the prime minister who appointed him (Lord Liverpool), that he was of a godly, temperate and conscientious disposition. Kaye was not socially well connected, and had no relevant parochial experience, so these factors, which would certainly have been relevant for many other bishops at this date, did not come into the equation. He saw himself as deeply embedded into the fabric of society, and the fact that he received vast quantities of correspondence from people at all levels of society suggests that this was a mutual recognition.[17]

Within the constraints of the expectations on leadership that pertained in his day, it is evident that Kaye sought to be a model of humility and to share oversight. He told the clergy in his first charge that they were meeting 'for the purposes of *mutual* instruction' (my italics).[18] He also made it clear that running his enormous diocese would be impossible without the support of his coadjutors, 'coadjutors to whom I could at all times resort in the certain assurance of receiving counsel, the result of profound learning, intimate acquaintance with the theory and practice of ecclesiastical law, sound judgement and well-tempered zeal for the interests of our Church; –

[16]   Kaye, *Nine Charges*, 311.
[17]   See Ambler's Introduction to *Lincolnshire Correspondence* for the most recent and detailed evaluation of Kaye's work.
[18]   Kaye, *Nine Charges*, 3.

coadjutors who by the weight of their authority would give effect to any plans which I might devise for ameliorating the spiritual condition of the diocese.'[19] He was referring to his archdeacons, who were, in the words of canon law, 'the eyes of the bishop'. At the outset, then, he made it clear that he saw the exercise of ecclesiastical authority as a shared enterprise, and not something that solely rested in himself. Throughout his episcopate he placed great emphasis on the archdeacons, and not a shred of criticism of them, private or public, has survived. Indeed, writing to the prime minister Robert Peel in 1835, about the archdeacon of Lincoln, Charles Goddard, he stated 'I am persuaded that but for him a large proportion of the Churches of the Archdeaconry would now be in ruins.'[20] All of his archdeacons had had significant parochial experience, and, lacking this himself, he respected it in them.

Equally importantly, Kaye was instrumental in reviving the office of rural dean in his diocese. Rural deans were trusted and experienced incumbent clergy, who had oversight within the deanery in which they resided, under the authority of the archdeacon. In practice, this meant supervising around ten parishes. They were supposed to provide a role model and support for the other clergy in their patch, and sort out, or circumvent, local disputes. They were also active in promoting church schools. It was an innovation that was both welcome and successful, and rural deans, or area deans, continue to this day.[21]

Kaye also believed that he required the support of other clergy in order to properly exercise his duties in relation to ordinands. A bishop, he wrote, 'needs, and is entitled to claim, the zealous co-operation of all his brethren in the ministry' when it came to weeding out those unsuitable for ordination.[22] Although he could make judgements about the academic fitness of ordinands, he knew that he 'must be for the most part dependent on the testimony of others to judge the moral fitness of candidates.'[23] He also put limits on episcopal power, declaring that a bishop should avoid being 'offensively inquisitorial' and should not question clergy or ordinands in a way which implied distrust.[24]

[19] Kaye, *Nine Charges*, 26–7.
[20] See British Library, Add Mss 40417f.235, Kaye to Peel, 19 March 1835.
[21] For a detailed discussion of the revival of rural deans within the Church of England, see Arthur Burns, *The Diocesan Revival in the Church of England c.1800–1870* (Oxford: Oxford University Press, 1999), 75–107.
[22] Kaye, *Nine Charges*, 64.
[23] Kaye, *Nine Charges*, 66.
[24] Kaye, *Nine Charges*, 76.

Was he, as Newman would have asserted, over reliant on an authority derived from the state? The answer is 'Yes and no'. He certainly believed that it was the duty of the state to support the work of the Church with relevant legislative measures, and in common with other high churchmen, he believed that the state was a divinely ordained institution. In the troubled year of 1831, however, he was clear eyed about the possibility of disestablishment. Even if the union with the state was dissolved, he said, the Church would remain 'as a congregation of faithful men, in which the pure Word of God is preached, and the sacraments duly administered according to Christ's ordinance ... no change in its external circumstances can affect the relation in which we stand to it'. It would continue as before, supported by its thousands of followers who assented to its creeds, and who loved 'its simple yet impressive ceremonies' and 'warm yet sober devotion', believing it to be a powerful instrument for the salvation of souls.[25]

If we were able to ask him what he thought he was doing, he might have replied that he was doing his best to minister to those who supported the Church by ensuring the provision of regular worship throughout his vast diocese, and an adequate supply of fairly competent resident clergy. He was making provision for numerous schools and was sharing the task of managing the diocese and its clergy with his trusted group of archdeacons and rural deans. He was upholding the principles of the Reformation, and the foundational texts of the Church of England, namely the Book of Common Prayer and the Thirty-nine Articles. He was seeking to chase out error, whether that came from Tractarians, Anglican evangelicals, Roman Catholics or Protestant Dissenters. He was doing his best to make the Church of England a more attractive proposition than any of the other forms of Christianity that were available.[26] Speaking in the House of Lords in 1828 in a debate about the legislation which opened Parliament fully to Protestant Nonconformists, a measure which he supported, he noted that 'the best security of the Church of England is the hold which it possesses on the esteem and affections of the people.'[27] It was an admission that its

[25]   Kaye, *Nine Charges*, 78–9.
[26]   He provides a summary of what he thought he had been doing during his twenty-five years in Lincoln in the closing pages of his final charge (Kaye, *Nine Charges*, 472–5).
[27]   John Kaye, 'A Speech on the Second Reading of the Bill for the Repeal of the Test and Corporation Acts', in the House of Lords, Thursday April 17, 1828.' At: https://hansard.parliament.uk/Lords/1828-04-17/debates/3114c153-9545-

authority was conferred, not only by the formal mechanisms of the crown and parliament, but also to some extent, by popular consent. This was a securer basis than seeking its validation through a particular reading of its own episcopal history.

4453-b635-d4c0ac0b9ad0/CorporationAndTestActsRepealBill (accessed 21 March 2022).

Episcopé in the EKD and the Church of England

*Why Ordination Rites and the Architecture of Governance Allow
for the Interchangeability of Ordained Ministers*

Peter Scherle

Introduction

The following paper argues for the interchangeability of ordained ministers
between the Church of England and the constituent churches of the EKD.[1]
Since it is the Church of England that has doubts as to whether the 'apostolic (historic) faith' is preserved by the ordering of the episcopate in the
EKD, I intend to show that ecclesial governance and shared oversight in
the churches of the EKD are an equivalent of the 'historic episcopate in
apostolic succession', which has become an identity marker of the Church
of England.[2] In very much the same way, it is necessary to address the

---

[1]   See: *Meissen Declaration: On the Way to Visible Unity. A Common Statement*, 18
        March, 1988 (Meissen 1988), 16.

[2]   Mark Chapman calls it 'the criterion for Catholic identity' (*Anglican Theology*
        (London: T&T Clark, 2012), 195). Jonathan Gibbs relates the identity-question to
        H. Richard Niebuhr's, *Social Sources of Denominationalism* (1929). He suggests
        that the publication of the revised Book of Common Prayer in 1662 was 'a defining
        moment in the formation of Anglican identity' and at the same time for the Church
        of England 'the beginning of its decline into a religious sect and the moment it lost
        its claim to be a truly catholic church' (149). Jonathan Gibbs, "A Way Ahead for
        Meissen?", in Mark Chapman, Friederike Nüssel,, Matthias Grebe, (eds), *Revisiting
        the Meissen Declaration after 30 Years* (Beihefte zur Ökumenischen Rundschau
        126) (Leipzig: Evangelische Verlagsanstalt, 2020), 145–155, 146–7. It would be
        helpful here to also remember the 'theory of collusion' (Kollusionstheorie) devel-
        oped in the Münster Ecumenical Institute in the 1970s, which understands ecu-
        menical processes as a complex interplay between three factors in the life of
        churches: (doctrinal) truth, (denominational) identity and (ecclesial) sociality. (The
        theory was presented in: Peter Lengsfeld, *Ökumenische Theologie. Ein Arbeitsbuch*
        (Stuttgart: Kohlhammer, 1980)). For a recent discussion see: Maria Wernsmann,
        *Praxis, Probleme und Perspektiven ökumenischer Prozesse. Ein Beitrag zur Theo-
        riebildung* (Beihefte zur Ökumenischen Rundschau), Leipzig: Evangelische Ver-
        lagsanstalt, 2016).

claims in the constituent churches of the EKD to represent a presbyterial-synodal (and consequently non-episcopal) model of church-governance, and to understand pastoral ministry as purely functional (and consequently non-sacramental), more as identity-markers than as church-dividing theological differences. In effect, mutual trust must be seen as central to the question of interchangeability of ordained ministers.

The argument will be developed in three steps: first, a detailed discussion of the architecture of governance in the EKD will demonstrate that there is an episcopal dimension to that architecture, fulfilling fundamentally the same function as the historic episcopate in the Church of England; both with respect to the '*potestas ordinis*' and to its task of preserving (or perhaps better expressed as proclaiming and protecting) the historic apostolic faith. (Differences concerning the involvement of the ordained ministry in the '*potestas regiminis*' depend on the respective state-church laws as well as the specific legal structures of ecclesial governance. These need not be seen as essential for the interchangeability of ministers). In the second step a closer look into the ordination liturgies helps us to realize that the EKD and the Church of England use the same liturgical grammar, which reveals that they both share a theology of ordination which is at the same time *functional* (to administer word and sacrament) and *sacramental* (ordination as an epicletic event by which the church's calling is imparted by and dependent on the Holy Spirit). In the third step we need to spell out the challenges that arise from these legal and liturgical reflections for the EKD and the Church of England, in order to build the necessary trust in each other's practice of episcopé.

The architecture of governance in the EKD (in relation to the Church of England[3])

The first part of this paper presents a sketch of the architecture of governance of the EKD (as inscribed in ecclesiastical law). It shows the historical development and interrelationship of four dimensions of governance:

---

[3]   The presentation by Augur Pearce (in 'The Expression of the Anglican Understanding of *Episkope* in the Law of the Church of England', in *Visible Unity and the Ministry of Oversight:* The Second Theological Conference held under the Meissen Agreement betweeen the Church of England and the Evangelical Church in Germany, West Wickham, March 1996 (London: Church House Publishing, 1997), 141–151) shows similarities and differences in the architecture of governance.

1) episcopal, 2) synodal and 3) consistorial held together in 4) collegial bodies of governance.[4] This architecture is rooted in the Reformation critique of the historic episcopate as it was practised at that time, when bishops held the *'potestas ordinis'* and the *'potestas regiminis'* at the same time (the latter of which included the *'potestas iurisdictionis'*, the *'potestas executionis'* and the *'potestas iudicialis'*). This form of ecclesiastical governance, according to the Reformers, did not protect the 'apostolic (historic) faith'.

The separation of the two *'potestates'* became essential to church order in reformation churches, as did a complex weaving together of the different forms of governance. While the *'potestas regiminis'* resided in the respective ruler as *'summus episcopus'* (at the same time in charge of the *'ius circa sacra'* and the *'ius in sacra'*), who governed the church with the help of consistorial colleges, in which theologians and lawyers worked together in the task of – what we should precisely call – 'organisational episkope'.[5] The *'potestas ordinis'* resided in the ordained ministry, whose task at all levels of Church was understood to be 'pastoral episkope'.[6] In fact, as ordination liturgies clearly show, every minister was ordained as (local) bishop, while some of them were installed in order to exercise regional pastoral episcopé.

The development of the synodal dimension in ecclesial governance is related to the development of modern democratic conceptions of sovereignty. While the Greek term *'synodos'* is an ancient way of describ-

---

[4]   On this see Thomas Barth, *Elemente und Typen landeskirchlicher Leitung* (JusEcc 53) (Tübingen: Mohr Siebeck, 1995); Dieter Kraus (ed.), *Evangelische Kirchenverfassungen in Deutschland. Textsammlung mit einer Einführung* (Berlin: Dunker & Humblodt, 2001); Wolfgang Huber, 'Synode und Konziliarität. Überlegungen zur Theologie der Synode', in G. Rau, H.-R. Reuter, and K. Schlaich (eds), *Das Recht der Kirche Band III. Zur Praxis des Kirchenrechts* (FBESG 51) (Gütersloh: Gütersloher Verlag, 1994), 319–348.

[5]   Jan Rohls (in 'Apostolicity, Episkope and Succession: The Lutheran, Reformed and United Tradition', in *Visible Unity*, 93–107, 96) summarizes this as follows: 'The local pastor is, therefore, the inheritor of the office of the bishop as a spiritual office-holder. On the other hand, it is the Prince as emergency bishop who takes over the functions in the governance of the Church which belonged to the bishop, and in the end it is to him that the superintendents are subordinated as officials.'

[6]   In medieval discussions bishops and presbyters shared the *'potestas in corpus eucharisticum'*, while the *'potestas in corpus mysticum'*, the 'power of rule or government in the church', began to be assigned to the bishop (Paul F. Bradshaw, *Rites of Ordination. Their History and Theology* [Collegeville/Minnesota: Liturgical Press, 2013, 142–3]).

ing the pilgrim church 'together on the way', the idea of freely elected members of a synod as a church governing body is dependent on the idea of the 'sovereignty of the people', as developed – with some influence from reformed covenant-theology[7] – in modern political thought. When the churches in Germany after 1918 were required to develop their own church order, the separation of the three powers (legislative, executive, juridical) in the tradition of Montesquieu's political thought became a model for the architecture of church government. Nowadays synods, composed of elected non-ordained (two thirds) and ordained members (one third), are responsible for ecclesiastical legislation as well as in the overall organisation and securing of pastoral oversight, which is exercised collegially by a body in which members of the synod, the administration, and the episcopacy (meaning those who hold the offices of bishops/church presidents and those who hold regional episcopal offices) work together under the presidency of the highest ranking ordained '*episcopos*'.

It is, nevertheless, also essential to this struture, that the ordained ministry is responsible for the 'pastoral oversight'[8] which derives from the responsibility for the proclamation of the Gospel in word and sacrament. Those who are ordained and 'installed' (licensed) ministers of the

---

[7] Rohls (in 'Apostolicity', 97–100) explains the difference between the Reformed and the Lutheran tradition: 'In Calvinism the spiritual power of the bishop may go to the pastors, which means the old *iure divino* superiority of the bishop over the pastors disappears, but by contrast with Lutheranism, the episcopal government of the Church goes not to the Prince as emergency bishop but to the synods. And the actual *episcope* is finally exercised by collegial bodies from the presbytery right up to the general synod' (100). While synods in the sixteenth century were composed of 'officials' and reflected an aristocratic form of governance, they were later transformed into democratic organs, composed of elected members. In fact, the churches in Germany 'are hybrids of two different forms of *episkope*, namely that of the Lutheran episcopal office of the Reformation period and that of the Calvinistic presbyterian-synodical church order. By contrast, a pure high-church episcopal model was no more able to prevail in German territorial churches after the collapse of the government of the Church by princes than was a pure Presbyterian-synodical model system' (105).

[8] The term 'ministry of pastoral oversight' (para 15 ix, *Common Statement*) is already introduced. In 'Ministry and the Office of Bishop according to Meissen and Porvoo: Protestant Remarks about Several Unclarified Questions' (in *Visible Unity*, 9–48, 38). Ingolf Dalferth, speaks correspondingly of a '*synodical episcopate*', in order to clarify that '*episkope* can *never be limited to ordained clergy*, but is in a quite decisive regard the concern of *congregations and synods*' (39).

church, share the task of handing on and protecting the 'historic apostolic faith' the church has received. Although the synod is responsible for the organization of the way in which the apostolic faith is handed on, the ordained ministers decide on what is preached and taught in the churches of the EKD. The 'right of the pulpit' is solely theirs, but with one exception: those who hold the office of an *'episcopos'* have the ancient episcopal right to preach from all pulpits of the respective church or region. And they also have, in personal or (episcopal-) collegial responsibility, the task of overseeing the continuity with the apostolic faith in the life of the church.

A fundamental tension is inscribed into this architecture of church government that is rooted in the self-understanding of Church as the body of Christ. On the one hand, as a social body, it engages with the concepts of sovereignty that are present in the 'body politic'.[9] Church order at all times and in all places can only use the political mechanisms available. None of them – be it monarchic, aristocratic, democratic or some form of 'post-democratic' governance – is given by divine institution. And they all assume a sovereignty that resides in a power that 'enforces' the will of the sovereign as represented in the respective organs of the body politic.[10]

On the other hand, the church as the body of Christ has to live with the sovereignty of God in Christ; a 'sovereignty' which it cannot 'represent,' but only await in the coming of Christ that transforms and heals all creation. The ordained ministry has the task of holding world and church open for this sovereignty from beyond.[11] It reminds the church of a power

---

[9]   On this, see Daniel Loick, *Kritik der Souveränität* (Frankfurter Beiträge zur Soziologie und Sozialphilosophie Band 17) (Frankfurt / New York: Campus, 2012); Robert Jackson, *Sovereignty. Evolution of an Idea* (Cambridge and Malden/Ma.: Polity, 2007). Of special interest for theology is the ground-breaking study by Ernst Kantorowicz, *The King's Two Bodies: A Study in Medieval Political Theology* (Princeton/N.J.: Princeton University Press, 2016 [first published 1957]).

[10]   There is a debate about the 'crisis of representation' in political theory that needs to be taken into account. See, for example, Carl F. Raschke, *Force of God. Political Theology and the Crisis of Liberal Democracy* (New York: Columbia University Press, 2015).

[11]   See Peter Zeillinger, 'Repräsentation einer Leerstelle, oder: Auszug ins Reale. Zur politischen Bedeutung des biblischen Exodus, der historisch nicht stattgefunden hat' in *Interdisciplinary Journal for Religion and Transformation in Contemporary Society* 2 (2018): 212–282. Zeillinger has demonstrated how the Exodus narrative de-legitimated any inner-worldly representation of the sovereignty of JHWH by a person (not even by Moses) or an institution. The narrative itself presents it as a

it cannot exercise or 'enforce', but only witness to (*'sine vi sed verbo'*).[12] This belongs to the *'esse'* of the Church and this is what 'pastoral episkope' is about.

No form of episcopacy can escape the tension that has just been described. The ordained ministry also participates in an 'organisational episkope' that belongs to synods and collegial bodies of governance. It must act out the tension, but in a specific way. The contribution of the episcopate to ecclesial governance, that is, the 'pastoral episkope', can be grouped under three activities: ordination, visitation and theological(/spiritual) orientation. It is its role to make sure that strategic decisions of synods and collegial bodies (and the way in which they are made operative) can be related back to the normative horizons opened up by the historic apostolic faith.[13]

blank space, which can only be filled by the narrative itself: *'The position of the king in the Exodus narrative is replaced by the position of the text* [author's italics]' (257; translation by PS/MC).

[12] Loick (in *Kritik*, 279–321) shows that the Jewish understanding of Torah and legal commandment established a theory of sovereignty that established 'an understanding of law without enforcement' (283) because until 1948 it was not associated with political power or a (nation-)state. He considers this to be part of the reason that Jewish political thinkers such as Hermann Cohen, Franz Rosenzweig, Walter Benjamin and Hannah Arendt were able to develop a 'critical theory of/without sovereignty' (310).

[13] The Reformation churches differed in the way in which they understood the diaconate. While in the Reformed tradition four offices (teacher, pastor, elder and deacons) were upheld, ecclesial reality condensed these offices into two: pastors (absorbing the office of teacher) and elders, who as responsible for the resources of the Church, including the distribution of wealth among the poor, were in fact carrying out the diaconical ministry (cf. Rohls, "Apostolicity", 98). The Lutheran tradition, while focussing on the one ministry of word and sacrament (the office simultaneously of pastor and teacher) never quite developed the diaconate as an office of ministry, but assigned the task in practice to church governing bodies (which are responsible for the distribution of resources) and – in modern times – to covenantal communities (Diakonissen- oder Bruderhäuser) or specialised professions.

The grammar of ordination liturgies (and the consequences for interchangeability)

In the second part of this paper I now move on to address the understanding of ordination in the EKD by going back to the ordination liturgy, following the old insight that the *lex credendi* and the *lex vivendi* of the church are encapsulated in the *lex orandi*.[14] This step is necessary because the Church of England has doubts about the validity of the ordination practised in the churches of the EKD. And we want to take the importance of the Ordinal for Anglican identity seriously. If we look closely at our ordination liturgies from an ecumenical perspective, it is possible to sketch a grammar of protestant ordination liturgies that is similar to that of episcopal churches with the orders of deacon, priest and bishop.[15] In making the grammar visible, it is possible to identify the differences in a more precise manner than just in doctrinal reflection.

Ordination liturgies in the context of the EKD[16] comprise the three dimensions *vocatio, benedictio and missio*, that are present in ordination

---

[14] See also: W. Taylor Stevenson, 'Lex Orandi – Lex Credendi', in: S. W. Sykes and J. Booty (eds.), *The Study of Anglicanism* (London: SPCK, 1988), 174–188. Ingolf U. Dalferth (in *Auf dem Weg der Ökumene. Die Gemeinschaft evangelischer und anglikanischer Kirchen nach der Meissener Erklärung* (Leipzig: Evangelische Verlagsanstalt, 2002), 95) points to the danger he observes in an Anglo-Catholic ecclesiology of assuming the liturgy to be theologically unambiguous. Instead he suggests that liturgy offers 'implicit aspects of consensus' for theological reflection.

[15] Bradshaw (in *Ordination Rites*, 105) points out how the place of ordination in the liturgy can reveal this grammar: 'In the Byzantine rite the ordination of a bishop is located at the very beginning of the Eucharist, and the new bishop is then expected to read the Gospel, preach and offer the oblation; a presbyter is ordained immediately after the entrance of the gifts, so that he may then fulfil his new liturgical role by participating in the eucharistic action, and a deacon at the end of the eucharistic prayer, so that he may then fulfil the diaconical function of assisting in the distribution of the consecrated elements to the communicants.'

[16] In 2012 the two denominational bodies UEK and VELKD in the context of the EKD introduced a common selection of liturgies (see *Berufung – Einführung – Verabschiedung* (Agende 6 für die Union Evangelischer Kirchen in der EKD / Agende IV, Teilband 1 der VELKD für evangelisch-lutherische Kirchen und Gemeinden), Bielefeld: Lutherisches Verlagshaus/Luther-Verlag, 2012), which gives ordination (and installation) liturgies in the EKD a more common shape. For fundamental considerations concerning the relation of faith and order see Albert Stein, 'Ordination', in G. Rau, H.-R. Reuter and K. Schlaich (eds), *Das Recht der Kirche Band III. Zur Praxis des Kirchenrechts* (FBESG 51) (Gütersloh: Gütersloher Verlag, 1994), 73–117.

liturgies, so to say, 'at all times and in all places'. At first the calling of the person by God (*'vocatio interna'*) and by the respective church (*'vocatio externa'*) is enacted through performance, including the formal making of oaths, both to the apostolic faith and the laws of the respective church. At the centre of the ordination liturgy we find an epicletic prayer with the laying on of hands by a person representing the episcopate, by which the ordination is performed as God's own action acclaimed by the worshipping community.[17] The mission to which the ordinand is sent, may also be made visible by symbols of the task he or she has taken on. Of central importance though is the performance of that *'missio'* in the act of preaching, ideally immediately following the ordination liturgy itself. In this act the newly ordained minister begins the work that he or she has been called to: to proclaim the Gospel and to remind the church of what it is – a *'creatura verbi'*.

In some constituent churches of the EKD ministers are ordained in groups in a central ordination liturgy, in which the acting *'episcopos'* preaches. In this case the ordinand performs his or her *'missio'* at a later installation ceremony, when inducted as minister of a parish. In those churches where ordination and installation take place in one service in the respective parish church, the newly ordained minister always preaches immediately after being ordained. Sometimes this is misunderstood as 'ordination into(!) a parish'. But in fact, it is an ordination by the church which takes place in a parish.

The Anglican Ordinal – and this needs to be noted – replaced the conferral of the paten and chalice (as signs of the priestly offering) with the conferral of the Bible, handed over to priests and bishops alike, and thereby signifying the proclamation of the Gospel (in word and sacrament) as the *'missio'* of both orders. In the ordination/consecration of bishops – who may be anointed with sacred oil ('signifying the role of leadership') – after the Giving of the Bible, additional symbols of office are conferred: the

---

[17]   Bradshaw (in *Rites of Ordination*, 59–60) proposes that the 'first part of the directions in *Apostolic Tradition* 2.1–4 originally looked something like this': 'Let him be ordained bishop who has been chosen by all the people and when he has been named and accepted, let all the people assemble together with the presbytery on the Lord's day. When all give consent, let the presbytery lay hands on him, and let all keep silence, praying in the heart for the descent of the Spirit.' And he points out: 'Moreover, the prayer implies that the bestowal of the Holy Spirit was effected by a fresh outpouring at each ordination in response to the prayer of the church and not by its transmission from ordainer to ordinand, as in later thought' (63).

episcopal ring, the pectoral cross, and the pastoral staff (though the last of these may also be conferred later in the context of the 'Sending out'). The assumption of a bishopric, which may take place in a separate installation service, is symbolized by sitting on the bishop's chair. Here churches in the EKD lack liturgical coherence, since, on the one hand, there are usually no symbols conferred for the ministry of pastor, while, on the other hand, Bishops/church presidents receive an 'episcopal cross,' lacking any ministerial significance. In the end, it is liturgically more significant that the ordinands in churches like mine (the Evangelische Kirche in Hessen und Nassau) immediately do what they are called to do: they preach the word of God, thereby enacting the faith-conviction that the church is a '*creatura verbi*'.

Overall it is important to note that in the EKD ministers are ordained as bishops.[18] There is no episcopal ministry as a separate order to which ministers are consecrated. The '*installatio*' of bishops follows the same Ordinal as the installation of ministers into a new parish. The difference between a bishop's consecration/ordination and installation/induction in the Church of England and the installation of bishops/church presidents in the EKD in the liturgy is principally visible in two ways: first, in the Church of England there is a rich symbolism for the '*potestas ordinis*' and the (regional) episcopal task that is undertaken. This does not raise a theological question and makes no difference to the practice of episcopé. The second difference – sometimes enacted in a separate liturgy – is related to the '*potestas regiminis*' as symbolized by additional elements enacting the assumption of a bishopric.

This is where the challenge posed to the understanding of the historic episcopate in the Church of England rests. In the ecclesial structure of governance in the Church of England as it stands bishops are part of a multidimensional form of governance in which the General Synod is responsible for legislation, where there are ecclesial courts independent from the bishop, and where the bishop has instruments for administering his/her tasks (from suffragan bishops and archdeacons to the multi-professional staff in diocesan headquarters). This is fundamentally different from

---

[18] See Dorothea Wendebourg, 'The Reformation in Germany and the Episcopal Office', in *Visible Unity*, 49–78, 51: 'That is to say, the episcopal office is none other than the office of pastor.' She continue: 'The episcopate therefore did not represent a separate order, but only a specific dignity and function (*dignitas et officium*)' (52); 'The person ordained thereby entered into an episcopal line of succession' (53).

the sovereign power of bishops in the Roman Catholic Church and very close to the architecture of church governance in the EKD.

The challenge posed to the churches in the EKD is the recognition of what the ordination liturgy reveals: *ordination is not just functional, but also sacramental.* This is most clearly expressed in the fact that ordination is a once and for all event:[19] it cannot be revoked nor can it be repeated.[20] But the exercise of the *'potestas ordinis'* is and remains dependent on a legal licence (stipendiary or non-stipendiary) by the particular church. The problem here is that German theology has been distracted for the last 150 years in trying to explain that ordination is not a sacrament in the same way as baptism and Eucharist, which are seen theologically as *'media salutis'.* Neither does the complete separation of Article 5 of the Augsburg Confession (where the 'ministry' of word and sacrament is called a 'divine institution') and Article 14 of the Augsburg Confession (the 'office' of ministry is a *'rite vocatus'*) make sense. The tension must rather be seen as theologically meaningful.[21] Following Johannes Hoff's proposal, this might allow for a protestant re-reading of the concept of 'apostolic succession'.

---

[19]   Bradshaw (in *Ordination Rites*, 138) reminds us: 'It was a fundamental principle of early Christianity that no one could be ordained to any ecclesiastical office without an attachment to a specific ministerial vacancy. ... This attachment was later called a "title", and ordinations without a title, "absolute" ordinations were prohibited.' In the West a change came about in the twelfth century, when the concept of the 'indelible character' (139-150) was adopted, which made 'absolute' ordinations possible.

[20]   This is an important point, as the *Waterloo Declaration* (2001) by the Anglican Church of Canada and the Evangelical Lutheran Church in Canada shows. The 'giving of this office is permanent: the bishops in both churches are ordained for life service of the Gospel in the pastoral ministry of the historic episcopate, although tenure in office may be terminated by retirement, resignation or conclusion of term, subject to the constitutional provisions of the respective churches' (B. Affirmations, 3). At: https://www.anglicancommunion.org/media/ 102184/waterloo_declaration.pdf (accessed 21 March 2022).

[21]   Dalferth (in 'Ministry', 36) writes: 'So in the Reformation understanding the ordained ministry is not *sacerdotium*, but *ministerium*, more precisely *ministerium verbi divini*, and as such "the exercising of the ministry which is entrusted to and laid upon the whole congregation". ... However, no-one can speak in the name of the whole Church in his own accord; rather, the right and the authority to do this must be conferred by the whole church. This is why the exercise of this particular ministry in the Church requires *ordination*, the orderly commissioning and authorization for the ministry of *public* proclamation. ... To this extent the ordained ministry as "a gift of God to his Church" (para 15 viii of the Common Agreement) is essential to the Church being the Church.'

In ordination we accept this ministry as given by God and handed down in its specific social forms organized by the churches through the ages. Apostolic succession is historical as a form of 'metonymy'.[22]

According to Hoff, 'metonymy' is a suitable concept for understanding ordination because it involves a contingent relationship to an origin event that is no longer available – it is absent and hidden. The sign of ordination in its enigmatic given-ness is 'pre-metaphorical.' Ordination touches on the mystery of the divine vocation. In turn, the laying on of hands under epicletic prayer can be understood as a sign of an 'apostolic succession' without the need for historical verification. Ordination as a liturgical act represents an 'apriori residue resistant to interpretation' which means 'that the Church receives its life-form "from elsewhere" (from an invisible "Lord")'.[23] This means that the same is true for ordination as for the unity of the Church: it 'cannot be "produced", but only metonymically "received"'.[24]

It seems to me that such an understanding of ordination, and thus of the personal episcopé, corresponds to an understanding of the church that does not allow it to be absorbed into its social functionality and the prevailing organizational systems. It is admittedly true that the church can make use of state, economic or social experiences, including their insights about leadership. But it must first and foremost understand itself theologically as a divine institution that receives its existence from elsewhere.

For the Meissen process it also seems important that the EKD keeps its promise about the status of ordination. Up to now it is still possible that non-ordained ministers-in-training or voluntary preachers preside at the Lord's table or preach regularly. The Church of England was rightly concerned about the theological proposal of the VELKD to speak of 'commissioning' as an alternative to, or alongside, the term 'ordination'.[25] Therefore it may be important to recognize that a number of churches in Germany are presently revising their position with respect to what was agreed on in Meissen.

---

[22] Johannes Hoff, 'Ist die Ökumene ein dogmatisches Problem? Die „successio apostolica" und die Grenzen theologischer Glaubenshermeneutik", *Theologie und Glaube* 95 (2005): 91–101 (translation in the text by P.S.).

[23] *Hoff*, 'Ist die Ökumene ein dogmatisches Problem?', 98.

[24] *Hoff*, 'Ist die Ökumene ein dogmatisches Problem?', 95.

[25] See *Allgemeines Priestertum, Ordination und Beauftragung nach evangelischem Verständnis*. Eine Empfehlung der Bischofskonferenz der VELKD (Texte aus der VELKD 130), Hannover 2004; Unfortunately this has not been clarified in the VELKD/UEK ordinal: *Berufung – Einführung – Verabschiedung*.

Our reconstruction of the architecture of ecclesiastical governance in the EKD and the episcopal dimension that it contains opens up the possibility to identify a form of episcopé that is ordered and able to secure the historic apostolic faith, which is what the historic episcopate in apostolic succession performs in the Church of England.

For further ecumenical discussion it seems necessary to make a distinction between pastoral and organisational episcopé. In the EKD and the Church of England shared oversight is based on a similar conviction: governance in the church is at the same time spiritual and temporal (with the latter including both legislative and executive power, while assigning judicial power to independent courts). Nevertheless, there is a specific episcopal task, based on the ministry of word and sacrament that we should call 'pastoral episcopé'. The ordained ministry is solely responsible for ordination, visitation and (spiritual/)theological orientation in the context of the historic apostolic faith, and thereby contributes to the 'organisational episcopé,[26] in which it also participates.

Both church traditions, however, have to face the contemporary challenge of thinking further about their understanding of sovereignty. This modern concept (based on the theories of Jean Bodin, Thomas Hobbes, Jean-Jacques Rousseau and Immanuel Kant) is challenged in various ways (from Walter Benjamin to Giorgio Agamben). The churches need to take these challenges seriously in acknowledging that any form of governance – in the context of nation-state sovereignty – and legal organisation is based on 'force'. The ordained ministry is a constant challenge to this by proclaiming the Gospel of a coming Sovereign, who cannot be represented in church and world. Pastoral episcopé is oversight from the perspective of Christ's advent and of the 'world to come'.

In analysing ordination liturgies of both church traditions, we were able to discover the similarity of the practice of ordination. The enactment of '*vocatio, benedictio* and *missio*' is based on the same liturgical grammar. In fact, we can see that all ministers of word and sacrament in the EKD are ordained as (local) bishops and may later be installed as (regional) bishops/church presidents.[27] Liturgical differences, such as the lack of

---

[26]   Dalferth (in *Auf dem Weg der Ökumene*, 145) proposes to call this a 'synodal episcopacy', which must be open for those who are not ordained.

[27]   Would it not be possible to call this ordination an '*effective* sign' of 'the Church's intention to be faithful to its apostolic calling' and of 'God's promise to the Church'

symbols to signify the pastoral/episcopal task or the temporal tasks which the ordained undertake, are relevant. But they do not justify the claim of some sort of '*defectus ordinis*' in the churches of the EKD, especially since in these churches ordinations have to be led by those who hold an episcopal office, in order to signify the apostolic succession in history.

At the same time, both church traditions need to reflect afresh on the epicletic character of ordination. In the EKD it is hidden under the pressure to negate the 'sacramental' character of ordination and to call the central act a 'blessing' with the laying on of hands. The theological presumption of Augsburg Confession § 5, that ordination – while it is an act of a specific church – is a 'divine institution' and dependent on the work of the Holy Spirit, is thereby blurred. In the act of ordination God calls ministers and bishops into apostolic succession (understood as 'metonymy') by the power of the Holy Spirit. This should be made more visible in ordination liturgies. In the Church of England, the epicletic character of ordination may be more visible in practice, but can be blurred theologically by the (Anglo-Catholic) claim of apostolic succession being historical in the sense that an uninterrupted chain of ordinations by bishops would secure the apostolicity of the church. If the chain is seen as the work of God by the power of the Holy Spirit,[28] it would be possible to see more clearly that God has equipped the church at all times and in all places with men and women whom we consider '*episcopoi.*'[29]

in the way Mary Tanner speaks about the historic episcopate in the Church of England? (See Mary Tanner, 'The Anglican Position on Apostolic Continuity and Apostolic Succession in the Porvoo Statement', in *Visible Unity*, 108–119, 115). Dalferth, (in 'Ministry', 41) claims: 'This means, however, that *the Protestant churches did not only remain apostolic as a whole, but they have never left or given up the apostolic succession with regard to the ordained ministry, but precisely the opposite – they have preserved and applied it*'.

[28] The Faith and Order Commission of the Church of England speaks of the 'recognition that the ordained ministry is a distinctive gift of the Spirit is part of what makes a church a true part of the Catholic Church' (Faith and Order Commission, *Recognition by The Church of England of Orders Conferred in Other Churches*, 21 February 2014: at: https://www.churchofengland.org/sites/default/files/2017 (accessed 21 March 2022). Why, then, should the ordained ministry in the EKD not be a gift of the Spirit?

[29] According to Paul Avis, these historical structures of apostolic continuity are fallible. 'They are effective signs of apostolic continuity as long as they remain faithful to the Gospel' (Paul Avis, 'Episcopacy in relation to the Foundation and Form of the Church', in Ingolf. U. Dalferth and Paul Oppenheim (eds), *Einheit bezeugen / Witnessing to Unity (Springe, 1999; Cheltenham, 2001)* (Frankfurt am Main: Lembeck, 2004, 121–134, 132–34). Christof Theilemann (in 'What Constitutes a

Summing up, then, the Church of England and the EKD should be able to take an important step towards visible unity by allowing full interchangeability of ordained ministers. All necessary arrangements concerning licensing and installation can be based on the mutual recognition of ordination in both church traditions.[30] But we should not forget that a step like this can be taken only if there is enough mutual trust.

Church?', in Chapman, Nüssel and Grebe, *Revisiting*, 21–27, 25) puts it in pneumatological language: 'The Church is apostolic in so far as the Spirit who takes care of the Gospel is active in the Church'.

[30] Whether this is considered possible depends on the understanding of the goal of 'full visible unity' and the interpretation of the theological key categories 'koinonia' and 'communio'. Dalferth (in *Auf dem Weg der Ökumene*, 15) argues quite rightly that the difference between the divine communion and our ecclesial forms of fellowship or community should not be blurred. Therefore 'full visible unity' is not something to be achieved by the churches, but to be received – in word and sacrament and, subsequently, in lived ecumenism (28) – as a divine gift that is present but remains as such invisible/hidden. The *'notae internae ecclesiae'* (Unity, Holiness, Catholicity and Apostolicity) are attributed to the Church – in the creed, which has its place in worship – as effected by God. They are witnessed to and represented (in the sense that the invisible is made visible as the invisible) in word and sacrament, i.e. the *'notae externae ecclesiae'*. Any form of church order – to introduce a third dimension into church theory – can only correspond to this in an imperfect manner. But it should at least not counter or contradict what is believed (*notae internae*) and celebrated (*notae externae*) in the churches. On this, see Peter Scherle, 'Kirche und Amt. Eine evangelische Sicht' in Joachim G. Piepke (ed.), *Die Kirche – erfahrbar und sichtbar in Amt und Eucharistie. Zur Problematik der Stellung von Amt und Abendmahl im ökumenischen Gespräch* (Veröffentlichungen des Missionspriesterseminars St. Augustin Nr. 55) (Nettetal: Steyler Verlag, 2006), 99–121. This can be called a weak reading of Article III of the Barmen Declaration of 1934. The strong reading of Barmen III, widespread in the constituent churches of the EKD, has pushed the idea of a 'missionary structure' [from the 1950s], the 'optimal organization' [from the late 1980's] and – now influenced by developments in the Church of England and following the influx of market-theories into church reform – a 'mixed economy'. This locks the churches into never-ending processes of restructuring, while avoiding a much more serious spiritual and theological crisis (cf. Ralf Meister, 'German Protestantism and the EKD in the years to come: theological visions, challenges and hopes', in Chapman, Nüssel and Grebe, *Revisiting*, 132–144, 142–144.).

Lambeth 1920, Bishops, and the Church of South India

Mark Chapman

This paper seeks to show how a particular understanding of the term 'historic episcopate' had come to define Anglicanism by the time of the Church of South India proposals of the 1930s, which had crucial implications for ecumenical relations between Anglicans and non-episcopal churches.[1] By this stage, the Anglican Communion had been recast into a denomination in which the 'historic episcopate' had become the key part of its identity, a move that has even been described as the 'episcopalization' of Anglicanism.[2] I also show that while there were alternative models to this sort of 'Lambeth Anglicanism'[3] which continued to regard Anglicanism as a form of Protestantism adapted for a particular context, these were supplanted by a fixation on the centrality of episcopacy as of the *esse* of the church.

---

[1]   'Proposed Scheme of Union', March 1929, in G.K.A. Bell (ed.), *Documents on Christian Unity*, Second Series (Oxford: Oxford University Press, 1930), 145. This paper draws on a much longer piece 'Anglican Ecumenism and the Problems of the "Historic Episcopate",' in Jane Platt and Martin Wellings (eds), *Anglican-Methodist Ecumenism: The Search for Church unity, 1920–2020* (London: Routledge, 2022), 29–46.

[2]   On this, see Steffen Weishaupt, 'The development of the concept of episcopacy in the Church of England from the nineteenth to the mid-twentieth centuries' (DPhil thesis, University of Oxford, 2013).

[3]   See Robert William Keith Wilson, *George Augustus Selwyn (1809–1878): Theological Formation, Life and work* (Farnham: Ashgate, 2010), 149–153.

A good illustration of this episcopalization of Anglicanism is offered by Frederic Hood (1895–1975), Principal of Pusey House, Oxford, which by that stage had established itself as a bastion of conservative Anglo-Catholicism in the University. In 1935 Hood published a strong defence of what might be regarded as a maximal understanding of the 'historic episcopate':

> The Historic Episcopate ... is of the very essence of the Church of England; and could not be suffered to be called in question by any body or individual desirous to be incorporated in our Communion.[4]

At least for a certain type of Anglo-Catholic, the historic episcopate alone functioned as the very centrepiece of Anglican self-understanding. The term had found its way into common usage in the Anglican Communion at the third Lambeth Conference of 1888, as one requirement for union with other churches, along with the Scriptures, the two dominical sacraments and the ecumenical creeds. Given that the other three points would be acceptable to all doctrinally-orthodox sacramental churches, it was the historic episcopate that was to become the key distinguishing feature of Anglican identity.

It is important to note, however, that there was no clarification of precisely what was meant by 'historic episcopate' at the 1888 Lambeth Conference. For many, such vagueness was unsatisfactory. In the years that followed, especially after the First World War, it was the Anglo-Catholic view that identified it in terms of apostolic succession that came to dominate thinking about the historic episcopate.

---

[4]   Frederic Hood, *Some Comments on the South India Scheme* (Westminster: Church Literature Association, 1935), 3. Hood is citing a former Bishop of Oxford, the historian, William Stubbs. See William Stubbs, edited by Ernest Edward Holmes, *Visitation Charges Delivered to the Clergy and Churchwardens of the Dioceses of Chester and Oxford* (London: Longmans, Green & Co., 1904), 130.

The claims of the Lambeth Quadrilateral were given an enormous boost following the famous Appeal of the 1920 Lambeth Conference,[5] which laid the foundations at an international level for Anglican ecumenism in the context of the post-First World War settlement. The emphasis was again on the episcopate as something to be graciously received through 'the apostolic rite of the laying-on of hands' (VII). While it did not deny the 'spiritual reality' of the ministry of those churches that did not possess episcopacy (VII), the Appeal nevertheless expressed the hope that 'would lead ministers who have not received it to accept a commission through episcopal ordination' (VIII).

For many in the Church of England in particular, the Anglican Communion was understood as the ecclesiastical equivalent of the nascent British Commonwealth as it began to develop into a federation of self-governing dominions.[6] The Lambeth Appeal amounted to a call for a kind of League of Nations for the churches so that denominations, including Anglicanism, at least in its limited Protestant and English form, would cease. There were other changes affecting ecumenism in the post-War world. Much of the earlier pan-Protestantism represented by many Anglicans in pre-War years through the appropriation of German liberal scholarship had run into the sands through the accusations of liberalism as guilty by association with Germany's war aims.[7] Following the War Anglo-Catholicism had risen to the ascendant.[8]

---

[5] 'An Appeal to All Christian People from the Bishops Assembled in the Lambeth Conference of 1920', (Resolution 9: Reunion of Christendom) at: https://www.anglicancommunion.org/media/127731/1920.pdf (accessed 10 February 2022).

[6] On this, see my essay, 'Un-Protestant and Un-English: Anglicanism and the 1920 Lambeth Conference "Appeal to All Christian People"', *Ecclesiology* 16 (2020), 159–74.

[7] See my *Theology at War and Peace: English Theology and Germany in the First World War* (London: Routledge, 2017); and 'William Sanday, Modernism, and the First World War', in Andrew Mein, Nathan MacDonald and Matthew A. Collins (eds), *The First World War and the Mobilization of Biblical Scholarship* (London: T & T Clark, 2019), 69–88.

[8] See Mark Chapman, 'The Church of England, Serbia and the Serbian Orthodox Church in the First World War' in Vladislav Puzovi (ed.), зборник радова са Међународног начног скупа Православни свет и Први светски рат [Proceedings of the Orthodox World and the First World War, 5–6 December 2014] (Belgrade: Faculty of Orthodox Theology, 2015), 385–401.

That said, one of the ironies of Anglican ecumenical involvement is that the commitment to church unity expressed in the Lambeth Appeal of 1920 was at the same time a strong affirmation of Anglicanism as an exclusive kind of church based on its allegiance to a particular understanding of the historic episcopate: the very impetus towards stating the minimum requirements for ecumenism helped shape a global denominational identity which made it far less willing to embrace its historic protestantism.

Mission, India, and Ecumenism

The main spur to ecumenical co-operation came from the problems that emerged alongside missionary expansion through the nineteenth century. Some of the key features that had originally set European churches and denominations against each other in such matters as church government or liturgical practice came to be seen as increasingly irrelevant in the completely new contexts represented in Africa as well as in south and east Asia. Some of the earliest efforts at ecumenical co-operation took place in India. In 1870, for instance, the Free Church of Scotland Indian convert, the Revd Lal Behari Day (1824–1892) had proposed a union for Bengal on the basis of Episcopal, Presbyterian and Congregationalist principles in order to free Christianity from what he regarded as its European forms that constricted the proclamation of the Gospel. In turn, by the outbreak of the First World War, reunion conferences were becoming more and more frequent as Anglicans and representatives of other denominations discussed possible routes towards reunion.

By 1919, the well-known Conference held at Tranquebar resulted in a Manifesto proposing a scheme for reunion agreed by Anglicans and members of the South India United Church which comprised of a union of Presbyterians and Congregationalists.[9] With the renewed emphasis on reunion after the Lambeth Appeal there were moves towards a more substantial set of proposals to bring about a new united church. In 1929 E. H. M. Waller (1871–1942) Bishop of Madras, noted that the Gospel im-

---

[9]   'Statement drawn up by Thirty-three Ministers of the Anglican and South India United Churches at Tranquebar, May 1 and 2, 1919', in G. K. A. Bell (ed.), Documents on Christian Unity: 1920-4 (Oxford: Oxford University Press, First Series, 1924), 278.

perative 'that all might be one' was the principal consideration.[10] The 'Proposed Scheme of Union', which was completed in March 1929, emphasised the role of the Spirit in promoting the 'bond of peace'.[11] The pattern of faith for the new church was identical to that of the Lambeth Quadrilateral and the Lambeth Appeal. Along with the centrality of Scripture, it would also require the acceptance of the Apostles' and Nicene Creeds, as well as the dominical Sacraments of Baptism and the Eucharist.[12] More complex, however, was the issue of church order, especially the Episcopate. While there was acceptance of 'the historic episcopate in a constitutional form as part of their basis of union', this did not mean that there was any intention 'thereby to imply, or to express a judgement on, any theory concerning episcopacy'.[13]

In formulating the final proposals Edwin James Palmer (1869–1954), Bishop of Bombay had long advocated the centrality of the historic episcopate for any unity. Ministers in the new church, he felt, should consequently 'accept a commission through Episcopal ordination'.[14] This point, however, was modified in 1926 which allowed the proposals to go forward but which caused significant problems for many Anglicans: until such time as all bishops and clergy conformed to the historic order there was to be a thirty-year interim period in which anomalies might be borne. Consequently, while in the long run all those in ministry would be episcopally-ordained ministers, there would be exceptions until that time.[15] The chief problem with the South India proposals was the interim period rather than the question of episcopacy *per se.*

Opposition

For opponents to these proposals the historic episcopate had come to be treated as an all or nothing affair: there could be no compromises, even for thirty years. Despite the acceptance of the centrality of episcopacy in

[10] E. H. M. Waller, *Church Union in South India: The Story of the Negotiations* (London: SPCK, 1929), 19.
[11] 'Proposed Scheme of Union', March 1929, in G. K. A. Bell (ed.), *Documents on Christian Unity*, Second Series, (Oxford: Oxford University Press, 1930), 145.
[12] 'Proposed Scheme of Union', 146.
[13] 'Proposed Scheme of Union', 146–147.
[14] Henry Whitehead, cited in Bengt Sundkler, *Church of South India: The Movement Towards Union 1900–1947* (London: Lutterworth Press, 1954), 63.
[15] 'Proposed Scheme of Union', 153.

the proposals, the interim measures meant that there were exceptions 'to the general principle of an episcopally ordained ministry'.[16] Even though former Anglican congregations would remain unaffected by the changes, the fact that there was the possibility of a church living with seeming anomalies was enough to ensure that the orders and sacraments of the whole church were open to question. According to Frederic Hood, the interim period contradicted the Preface of the Ordinal of the Book of Common Prayer as well as the Constitution of the Church of India, Burma and Ceylon.[17] Furthermore, it also ruled out the holy grail of union with Rome.[18] Consequently, he claimed, 'Great harm will be done to the very cause which we all have at heart, if this scheme is approved without drastic revision'.[19] This sort of opposition reveals that the South India proposals on episcopacy, however limited they were in practice, functioned as a red rag to the Anglo-Catholic bull: the very identity of the Church was at risk.

For many Anglo-Catholics, episcopacy had come to function as the guarantee of the church's authority against any encroachment either from an increasingly secular state or from other denominations. As N. P. Williams (1883–1943), Lady Margaret Professor of Divinity at Oxford and one of the leading academic spokesmen for Anglo-Catholicism of his day, put it: 'I venture to suggest that such a geographically-conditioned priesthood', as proposed in South India, 'would be practically as productive of irritation as it would be theoretically incapable of justification'.[20] For many, there was a fear that it marked the thin end of the wedge as the irregularity of non-episcopally-ordained clergy presiding over eucharists might set the pattern for future developments elsewhere, even possibly in England.

One of the harshest critics of the proposals was the poet T. S. Eliot who attacked what he regarded as the denial of Christian truth which could never be dependent purely on context. Furthermore, what happened on one side of the globe could easily affect the church at home:

---

[16] 'Proposed Scheme of Union', 153.

[17] Hood, *Some Comments*, 4.

[18] Hood, *Some Comments*, 8.

[19] Hood, *Some Comments*, 2.

[20] N. P. Williams, *Lausanne, Lambeth and South India: Notes on the Present Position of the Reunion Movement* (London: Longmans, Green and Co., 1930), 43.

Between the "missionary field" and the "home field" there can be no radical difference ... If it is accepted in India, it will inevitably be proposed in England. Not only logic will compel it, but circumstance. A precedent will have been established; the inconsistency will become intolerable; and we shall be told that if we do not conform to the precedent of India, it is we who will be responsible for the consequent disorder.[21]

The support that had been given by some English Churchmen to the proposals raised the question of 'whether the Church of England shall survive or perish'.[22] In particular, the thirty year interim period was nothing more than an 'amiable masquerade'[23] and would deny the ideal of 'a National Church' representing all people. In short, he concluded, 'As a Church, it would be only a shell'.[24]

Another variety of Anglican Ecumenism

At the same time, however, many Anglicans held a quite different understanding of the historic episcopate. This became apparent at one of the most important early international missionary conferences which took place in London in 1888 shortly before the Lambeth Conference at which Anglican attendance was limited to the evangelical Church Missionary Society. In a paper on Missionary Comity, C. C. Fenn (1823–1913), CMS Secretary from 1864-1891 noted that although there were 'great varieties of church government', all Christians were understood as 'belonging to the same outward visible Church'.[25] According to Fenn, 'those sectional differences among Protestant Christians, which are purely owing to historical causes or to local causes, will disappear among converts gathered in bodies so divided, if the converts act for themselves in countries where those historical or local causes are inoperative'.[26]

---

21   T. S. Eliot, *Reunion by Destruction: Reflections on a Scheme for Church Union in South India* (Council for the Defence of Church Principles, Pamphlet 7) (London: The Pax House, 1943), 5–6.
22   Eliot, *Reunion by Destruction*, 1.
23   Eliot, *Reunion by Destruction*, 12.
24   Eliot, *Reunion by Destruction*, 20–21.
25   C. C. Fenn, 'Missionary Comity', in James Johnston (ed.), *Report of the Centenary Conference on the Protestant Missions of the World*, 9th-19th June 1888 (London: Nisbet, 1889, 2 vols, 2, 470–477.

Fenn recognised that there would obviously be many repercussions for denominational self-identity from such an approach, most especially the different polities expressed in the various denominations which ranged from episcopal to independent. However, while recognising that Church Government would remain a problem, he nonetheless made some practical suggestions:

> The unity that exists among the Nagercoil Christians might be manifested by an annual or half-yearly gathering of ministers and lay delegates in a Congregational Union, presided over by a president chosen at each occasion. The corresponding body in Tinnevely might be a Central Church Council, presided over by a bishop. But the two central representative bodies might each regard the other as representing a part of the visible Church.[27]

Fenn also felt that the same sort of solution would apply to Presbyterians: 'The difference in Church government would not really break or even obscure their visible and evident union'.[28] Fenn cited the widely read New Testament scholar, Bishop J. B. Lightfoot: 'In the epistles of Ignatius there is no indication that he is upholding the Episcopal against any other form of Church Government, as, for instance the Presbyteral'.[29] Lightfoot had maintained that church orders were simply 'aids and expedients' which even though 'a Christian could not afford to hold lightly or to neglect', they 'were no part of the essence of God's message to man in the Gospel'.[30]

While the breakdown of Presbyteral government might have been best for the early church, Fenn observed, its replacement with Episcopal government was not something that could have universal validity for all time. He noted:

> Among the more progressive Christian countries of the world, the non-monarchic element of civil government seems, on the whole, at the present moment to be growing stronger and stronger. And, therefore, it would almost seem as

---

[26]   'Missionary Comity', 473
[27]   'Missionary Comity', 474
[28]   'Missionary Comity', 475
[29]   J. B. Lightfoot (ed.), *The Apostolic Fathers, Second Part, Vol. 1* (Epistles of St Ignatius) (London: Macmillan, 1885), 382, cited in 'Missionary Comity', 475.
[30]   J. B. Lightfoot, *Philippians* (refs to 6th ed. London: Macmillan, 1881), 184.

if the self-same cause which at one time led to the introduction of Episcopacy, might now have a tendency in the exact opposite direction.[31]

Fenn concluded by predicting a church that would embrace diversity in which 'great varieties of Church government will co-exist'. In such a church all would 'recognise each other as belonging to the same outward visible Church, the union being manifested by some corporate and representative action, and by very free intercommunion'.[32]

Conclusion

Fenn's view was obviously quite distinct from the view maintained by the bishops gathered at the Lambeth Conference of 1888 and even more so in 1920. It was also quite distinct from what was eventually adopted in the Church of South India. What Fenn's missionary example reveals is that 'Lambeth Anglicanism', or the establishment of a denomination founded solely on a particular theology of bishops, which has become the Anglicanism of ecumenism, is only one variety among the diversity of historical Anglicanisms.[33] However, it has come to be treated with such a degree of reverence and finality that alternatives, which were maintained by such key Anglican theologians as J. B. Lightfoot, have hardly ever been brought to the ecumenical table. Thirty years ago, the American Episcopal theologian William Countryman returned to something like Fenn's understanding:

> The goal of ecumenical unity requires a network of ordinations using bishops in the classic manner, but also deliberately and expressly preserving all of our existing ministerial successions. In such a network, we shall be speaking sacramentally both of our past, with its divisions, and a present in which unity is being reclaimed as our divine birthright. The resulting commingled succession will serve the future as a kind of sacramental recapitulation both of the griefs of the past and of God's grace in overcoming them. As such, it

---

[31] 'Missionary Comity', 476.
[32] 'Missionary Comity', 476.
[33] I have charted elsewhere the sorts of stories different Anglicans have told themselves about the nature of their identity. See *Anglican Theology* (London: T & T Clark, 2012).

may even come to seem a succession preferable to all its predecessors because it is richer in testimony to God's goodness to us.[34]

A Lambeth Conference solely comprised of bishops, however, is hardly likely to make much of such ideas, even if a 'commingled succession' is what ecumenism with protestant denominations seems to require. But logic and identity are seldom straightforward partners in ecumenical dialogue.

[34] L. William Countryman, *The Language of Ordination* (Philadelphia: Trinity Press International, 1992), 100–101.

Principles of Apostolic Ministry and Succession from a Lutheran Perspective

Friederike Nüssel

When the Evangelical Church in Germany (EKD) was founded at the Conference of Churches in Treysa on 31 August 1945, it was intended as a federation and organizational union of the Lutheran, Reformed and United regional churches in Western Germany. It attained its full legal form as a federation of churches with the adoption of the Basic Order (*Grundordnung*) on 13 July 1948 in Eisenach. Although the East-West conflict that developed soon after the end of the Second World War and the division of Germany immediately put the federal relationships in the young EKD to the test, it was nevertheless able to maintain its organizational cohesion until the construction of the Berlin Wall in 1961 and its legal unity until 1968, the year in which a new constitution for the GDR came into force and the eight eastern member churches had to establish their own federation of churches. For more than two decades, it was the only functioning large-scale church organization in the GDR. The special fellowship of all Protestant Christians in Germany was also emphasized in the order of the Federation of Protestant Churches in the GDR, which was founded in 1970, uniting with the EKD after German reunification in 1991 through the revival of the membership of its member churches, which had been dormant since 1969.

This brief history may indicate the importance of the federation for the relationship and communication between the Protestant Churches in Germany who share the heritage of the Reformation in Wittenberg. Since the individual *Landeskirchen* are autonomous ecclesial bodies with their own territorial history and identity in the Holy Roman Empire of German Nations, it was most important for communion among member churches of the EKD that they not only agreed on the understanding of the Gospel in line with the doctrine of justification and recognized baptisms, but that they were able to achieve communion in an understanding of the Eucharist and have exchangeability of ministers. Full eucharistic communion between all member churches was, after a first attempt through the Arnodshain Theses, achieved with the Leuenberg Concord only in 1973. The exchange of ministers was possible because all churches mutually recognize ordinations. However, at the same time, they live with a diversity in the order of *episkopé* because Lutheran and some United churches have the episcopal office, whereas other United churches and the Reformed churches have a *Kirchenpräsident* or *Präses*.

In earlier discussions, the Theological Conference of the Church of England and the EKD has discussed the convergences and remaining differences in the understanding of visible unity and apostolic succession in great detail.[1] While the remaining differences in the understanding of the ministry of oversight in apostolic succession still prevent full visible unity in terms of the interchangeability of ministry, one possible way of rereading the Meissen agreement and achieving interchangeability of ministry might be to reach a consensus on some kind of legitimate diversity in the interpretation of the role of the historic episcopate for apostolic succession. Such a rereading presupposes our churches can recognize in each other's order and exercise of *episkopé* the preservation and application of the principles of apostolic succession. The goal of this paper is to describe the principles of apostolic succession indicated in the Augsburg Confession and systematically explored in the Lutheran theology of Johann Gerhard in order to demonstrate how they allow EKD-churches and Lutheran churches elsewhere mutually to recognize the ministries of oversight and to accept a legitimate diversity in the order of *episkopé* in conversation with other episcopal and non-episcopal churches.

---

[1]   Church of England and Evangelical Church in Germany, *Visible Unity and the Ministry of Oversight. The Second Theological Conference held under the Meissen Agreement* (London: Church House Publishing, 1997); Ingolf U. Dalferth and Paul Oppenheim (eds), *Witnessing to Unity. Ten years after the Meissen Declaration* (Frankfurt am Main: Otto Lembeck, 2003); Christopher Hill, Matthias Kaiser, Leslie Nathaniel and Christoph Schwöbel (eds), *Communion already shared and further steps* (Frankfurt am Main: Otto Lembeck, 2010).

1. Tota ecclesia – the church as a whole is responsible for apostolicity

The central goal of the sixteenth-century Reformation was to renew the church as a whole in its apostolic mission. In article VII of the Confessio Augustana, Philipp Melanchthon states that the "one holy church is to continue forever." The reason behind this continuity lies in the fact that the church is the 'congregation of saints, in which the Gospel is rightly taught and the Sacraments are rightly administered.'[2] Only when these two elements are maintained can the Church claim to be apostolic. Consequently, it was Melanchthon's ecumenical agenda at the imperial Diet of Augsburg to achieve agreement over the essential conditions of apostolicity in order to preserve the unity of the Church. He argues that 'to the true unity of the Church it is enough to agree concerning the doctrine of the Gospel and the administration of the Sacraments,'[3] since it is through the proclamation of the Gospel in preaching and in the celebration of sacraments that God communicates God's unconditioned grace to be received by faith alone. While Melanchthon's ecumenical agenda for an apostolic Church was not successful in the theological negotiations between the reformers and the representatives of the Roman church, it became the basis and principle of Lutheran ecclesiology and the doctrine of ministry. While Wittenberg and the Swiss reformers became divided over the understanding of the Eucharist, the doctrine of incarnation and the doctrine of predestination, they shared the conviction that the apostolicity and the unity of the church depend on the right teaching of the Gospel and the right administration of sacraments. This agreement about the criteria of apostolicity, in turn, helped unification processes between Lutheran and Reformed churches in Germany in the nineteenth century and on the European level in the Communion of Protestant Churches in Europe based on the Leuenberg Concord (1973)[4] in the twentieth century.

The first and fundamental principle of Lutheran and Reformed ecclesiology became what I call the *tota ecclesia*-principle which means that the whole church and not only clergy is responsible for the apostolicity of

---

2   See https://bookofconcord.org/augsburg-confession/article-vii/ (accessed 21 March 2022).
3   Ibid.
4   Michael Bünker and Martin Friedrich (eds.), *Konkordie reformatorischer Kirchen in Europa (Leuenberger Konkordie) / Agreement between Reformation Churches in Europe* (Leipzig: Evangelische Verlagsanstalt, 2013).

the church. It was the Lutheran theologian Johann Gerhard (1582–1637) in Jena who promoted this principle in his ecclesiology and doctrine of ministry which he developed in his *Loci Theologici* in an intense debate with Robert Bellarmine (1542–1621) and his critique of Reformation doctrine and the church.[5] Building on Martin Luther's insight about the priesthood of all believers, Gerhard claimed that it is essential that not only the clergy, but the *tota ecclesia* has responsibility for the apostolicity of the church.[6] Whereas Luther stressed the priesthood of all believers in his teaching, that all baptized believers through their explicit faith are able to judge teaching and take responsibility for the apostolicity of the church,[7] Gerhard argued that while the whole church is responsible, only ordained ministers are called to and responsible for public teaching. In order to explain the participation and responsibility of all members of the church for the apostolicity of the church, Gerhard uses Luther's distinction between the three estates (*status ecclesiasticus*, *status politicus*, and *status oeconomicus*) through which God has ordered society for the sake of human flourishing. The *status ecclesiasticus* and the *ministerium ecclesiasticum* have been ordered by God to serve the promotion of eternal salvation and to fend off heresies and corrupt teachings. The other two estates are indirectly assigned to this goal. While the *status oeconomicus* in terms of marriage and family serves the propagation of the human race and the control of evil inclinations, the *status politicus* in terms of political government has to defend life and limb and to resist all kinds of tyranny. To Bellarmine's accusation of the Lutheran church as a *confusa multitudo*, Gerhard responds that through the Reformation, the original order of the Church had been restored in such a way that it offers a most pleasant sight to the spiritual eye as a shrewdly and carefully used and ordered structure in the in-

---

5   For a detailed analysis of Johann Gerhard's teaching on ministry see Friederike Nüssel, 'Zum Verständnis des evangelischen Bischofsamtes in der Neuzeit', in: Dorothea Sattler and Gunther Wenz (eds.), *Das kirchliche Amt in apostolischer Nachfolge, Bd. 2: Ursprünge und Wandlungen*, DiKi 13 (Freiburg i. Br. / Göttingen: Vandenhoech und Ruprecht, 2006), 145–189, see esp. 145–163.

6   See Johann Gerhard, *Loci theologici cum pro adstruenda veritate cum pro destruenda quorumvis contradicentium falsitate per theses nervose solide et copiose explicati*. Edited by Eduard Preuss, Vol. V (Berlin 1867). See here Locus XXIII. De Ministerio ecclesiastico, Cap. III/1, n. 71, 45a.b

7   See Friederike Nüssel, 'Amt und Ordination bei Martin Luther und in der lutherischen Dogmatik', in Felix Körner SJ and Wolfgang Thönissen (eds), *Vermitteltes Heil. Luther und die Sakramente* (Leipzig: Evangelische Verlagsanstalt, 2018), 143–161, 145–148.

teraction of the three estates in general and the order of ecclesial ministry in particular.[8] Although this harmonious vision of a Christian society lost its persuasive power in the course of the Thirty Years' War and the division between civil society and religion developed, the idea that all members of society are called to Christian witness in their very profession was preserved in the Protestant ethics of the professions[9] and entailed not only a secularization of ethics, but also a sacralization of the secular sphere.[10]

While Gerhard promoted the *tota ecclesia*-principle by way of what might be called an ecclesial sociology, the full potential of this principle entailed in Luther's doctrine of the priesthood of all believers could only be discovered and realized when the sovereign church regime came to an end in Germany in 1918. This presented the opportunity for the churches to bring the responsibility of all believers for the apostolicity of the church to bear at the level of church government through the formation of the synodical structure. Only then could the *tota ecclesia* principle be implemented for all church members through representative participation in church governance on regional and local levels.

2. Nisi rite vocatus – responsibility for the apostolicity in public teaching

The Augsburg Confession Art. XIV declares 'that no one should publicly teach in the Church or administer the Sacraments unless he be regularly called.'[11] While all believers are called to witness to the Gospel in consoling

---

[8]   Gerhard, Introduction to Locus XXIII, 1a: 'ita quoque ecclesia Spiritus s. charismasi in membris suis a Christo justitiae sole pulcherrime exornata conspectum sui exhibet spiritualibus oculis longe suavissimum, cum non sit confusa quaedam multitudo et colluvies, sed aciei probe instructae, ordinatae et vexillis certis distributae faciem obtineat.'

[9]   Cf. Ernst Troeltsch, 'Luther, der Protestantismus und die moderne Welt' (1907/08), in Ernst Troeltsch, *Gesammelte Schriften*, Vol. 4 (Tübingen: J. C. B. Mohr (Siebeck), 1925), 202–254, here 210: 'Die christliche Tugend der Selbst- und Weltverleugnung und der Bruderliebe sollte geübt werden mitten in der Welt und in den Formen des ständigen Berufs, dem ein jeder nach seiner Herkunft treu bleiben sollte … denn ein jeder führte nun das Doppelleben der persönlichen christlichen Tugend der Selbstverleugnung, Leidensfreude und Bruderliebe einerseits, der weltlichen Standes- und Berufspflichten andererseits.'

[10] See Volker Drehsen, 'Neuprotestantismus', TRE 24 (1994), 369, 58–370, 1.

[11] https://bookofconcord.org/augsburg-confession/article-xiv/ (accessed 21 March 2022).

their neighbours, the distinct character of ordained ministry consists in the responsibility for public teaching in preaching the Gospel and administering the sacraments. The proclamation of the Gospel in worship is, in the words of Luther, a public appeal to faith and Christianity (*'eyne offentliche reytzung zum glauben und zum Christenthum'*),[12] and the public which ordained ministry addresses in preaching the Gospel and administering the sacraments is in principle unlimited.[13] However, the public role of ordained ministry is even more complex, since the public proclamation of the Gospel addresses not only single believers as individuals, but gathers together a community of believers to become part of the body of Christ, and in this way works towards a particular public which is united in listening to the word of God.

In the controversies with Bellarmine, Johann Gerhard defended the rite of ordination as a condition for public teaching in contrast to Anabaptists, New Photinians and Socinians whom Bellarmine associated with Lutherans. Gerhard finds the biblical foundation for the necessity of ordination in Rom 10:15 ('let no one preach who has not been sent') and similar statements, but his historical view and corresponding exegetical method also requires him to demonstrate that the ritual of commissioning a person can be traced back across the Old and the New Testament. Gerhard's theological concern is to argue that ordination is based on a special divine vocation which has to be distinguished from the general vocation of all believers through baptism. Special vocation is the final reason for the authority of ordained ministers. Having argued as much, Gerhard adds a chapter about the vocation of Luther in response to Bellarmine's accusation that Luther had not received either an ordinary or an extraordinary vocation from God. The very fact that the paragraph on the vocation of Luther[14] became a regular part of the Lutheran doctrine of ministry in the seventeenth century, testifies to the importance of regular vocation through ordination as a formal condition of public ministry. For Gerhard and other Lutheran theologians of the time, it was not enough to argue that Luther's Reformation teaching was scriptural and led back to the teaching and practice of the early church; rather, he also thought it necessary to justify Luther's authority as an ordained minister on the basis of his divine calling and his ordination by a bishop.

---

12   Martin Luther, 'Deudsche Messe und ordnung Gottis diensts' (1526), *WA* 19, 75.
13   See Reiner Preul, 'Öffentlichkeit', RGG⁴ 6 (2003), 489–491.
14   See Gerhard, Locus XXIII, Cap. III/8, 83–90.

To defend the vocation and ordination of Luther, however, is only a tertiary concern in Gerhard's argument for the order of ministry in the Lutheran church. The real challenge from Bellarmine consisted in the denial of the validity of ordination because of the lack of historic episcopal succession. In his refutation, Gerhard employs two theological reasons which have become principles in the Lutheran teaching on ministry: first, the argument from the unity of ecclesial ministry; second, the distinction between personal or local succession and doctrinal succession.

3. The unity of ecclesial ministry

According to Art. VII of the Augsburg Confession, the existence of the church depends on public proclamation of the Gospel preaching and administration of sacraments. The proclamation of the Gospel in audible and visible words is God's way to call people to believe in him, to recognize his justice, and to trust his mercy which he has revealed in Jesus Christ in the power of the Holy Spirit. Similarly, Art V declares that God has 'instituted the Ministry of Teaching the Gospel and administering the Sacraments'.[15] According to the Lutheran understanding, this ministry of teaching the Gospel and administering the sacraments are essentially one. The Reformers, and later Johann Gerhard, found the source for this understanding in the New Testament according to which *episkopoi* are entrusted with the public proclamation of the Gospel as well as in the patristic understanding of the *episcopus* as a pastor of a congregation (especially in Jerome). The theological reason why there is only one ordained ministry of public teaching lies in the fact that the Gospel is essentially one.[16] It is the one Gospel which constitutes the church, and therefore the church is one. Hence, the ministry of public proclamation must also be one in the very essence of its mission, and *episkopé* is given in and through the vocation and the power to proclaim the Gospel in public. In exercising his *episkopé*, the pastor of a parish serves as *episkopos*, and the *episkopos* is essentially a pastor.

---

[15] https://bookofconcord.org/augsburg-confession/article-v/.(accessed 21 March 2022).

[16] See Melanchthon's position paper on the Regensburg book, CR 4, nr. 2254. The quotation can be found in Dorothea Wendebourg, 'The Reformation in Germany and the Episcopal Office', in *Church of England and Evangelical Church in Germany, Visible Unity and the Ministry of Oversight. The Second Theological Conference held under the Meissen Agreement*, 49–78, see endnote 42 on p. 70.

At the same time, while affirming the essential unity of ordained ministry, Luther, Melanchthon and the other Reformers in Wittenberg did not deny the distinction between bishop and pastor/presbyter that had been developed in the early church when Christianity expanded and an office of regional oversight became necessary to hold local congregations together. In former conferences, Dorothea Wendebourg has explained this in detail.[17] Even though the distinction between the office of bishop who has oversight over a region and the office of a local pastor cannot be derived from the New Testament and in the eyes of Reformation theology is a distinction *iure humano*, the ministry of oversight through visitation and ordination is understood as being necessary for the church.

The reason why the principle of the unity of ministry is important for the question of apostolic succession is twofold. First, it points to the intimate connection between ministry and the unity of the Gospel as the source of apostolicity. The church is *creatura verbi*, built on and living from the Word of God, and therefore the existence of the church is dependent on the ministry of public proclamation. This ministry has to be organized according to local and regional responsibilities, whereby the distinction between the episcopal and presbyteral office remains consistent and necessary. However, for the apostolicity of the church, the public proclamation is decisive, and this ministry is essentially one whether exercised by a bishop or a pastor. Second, the unity-principle explains why presbyteral ordination is theologically legitimate and valid, which again is important for the apostolicity of the church and for apostolic succession in situations when episcopal ordination is not available. Although Luther, Melanchthon and later Gerhard affirmed, in line with the patristic tradition, that ordination should normally be celebrated by bishops, the essential unity of ministry allowed them to organize presbyteral ordinations after 1535 when there were not enough pastors available to ensure the proclamation of the Gospel in parishes. While '[d]uring the first years of the Reformation, many priests and monks became Lutheran ministers, so that enough pastors were available,'[18] no bishops in the territory of the Holy Roman Empire were willing to ordain pastors who were adherents of

---

[17]　See Dorothea Wendebourg, 'The One Ministry of the One Church', in Hill et al, *Witnessing to Unity*, 300–323.

[18]　See Lutheran-Roman Catholic Commission on Unity, *From Conflict to Communion. Lutheran-Catholic Common Commemoration of the Reformation in 2017* (Leipzig: Evangelische Verlagsanstalt, 2013), nr. 66, 32.

the Reformation.[19] In this situation of 'pastoral emergency,' Luther and Melanchthon, while affirming episcopal ordination as the rule, saw the theological and pastoral priority in ensuring the Gospel would be preached to the people. The international Lutheran-Catholic discussion included the explanation of this procedure in the common narrative of the Reformation which they elaborated as the basis of the common commemoration of the Reformation in 2017. Part of this common narrative is the description of how the ordinations were organized in a way to demonstrate the catholic dimension of ordination: 'Ordinations took place in Wittenberg rather than in the parishes of the ordinands, since the ministers were ordained to the ministry of the entire church. The ordination testimonies emphasized the ordinands' doctrinal agreement with the catholic church. The ordination rite consisted in the laying on of hands and prayer to the Holy Spirit.'[20]

4. Doctrinal consensus as the heart of apostolic succession and the sign of episcopal ordination

In the Porvoo Common Statement,[21] by which Anglican and Lutheran Churches in Northern Europe were able to reach full visible unity and enter church communion, a fundamental agreement consists in the idea that apostolic succession characterizes the church as a whole. The manifestation of such apostolic succession has two dimensions: first, the 'primary manifestation of apostolic succession is to be found in the apostolic tradition of the Church as a whole. The succession is an expression of the permanence and, therefore, of the continuity of Christ's own mission in which the Church participates.'[22] A second dimension is to be found in the 'apostolic succession of the ministry which serves and is a focus of the continuity of the Church in its life in Christ and its faithfulness to the words and acts of Jesus transmitted by the apostles.'[23] This second dimension involves personal and local succession and episcopal ordination as a sign of local

---

[19] Cf. Dorothea Wendebourg, 'The Reformation in Germany and the Episcopal Office', 55–62.
[20] From Conflict to Communion, n. 68, 32.
[21] At https://www.anglicancommunion.org/media/102178/porvoo_common_statement.pdf (accessed 21 March 2022).
[22] Porvoo Common Statement, § 39.
[23] Porvoo Common Statement, § 40.

and personal continuity. From a Lutheran perspective, it is interesting to see that the distinction of the two dimensions of apostolic succession corresponds with Johann Gerhard's account of apostolic succession which he gives in response to Robert Bellarmine's doctrine of the necessary characteristics (*notae ecclesiae*) of the apostolic church and his critique of the Lutheran church for not maintaining the historic apostolic succession.[24]

Gerhard distinguishes between doctrinal succession, on the one hand, and personal and local succession, on the other, in order to identify the substantial source of apostolicity. He defines doctrinal succession as the internal dimension of apostolic succession and as the soul of the true church. Conversely, personal and local succession is for him an external dimension of succession. In order to categorize the relation between both dimensions of succession he uses the distinction between substance and accidents. While doctrinal succession is the substance of succession which consists in the doctrinal consensus that unites the church in its catholicity across generations and places, personal and local succession is the external dimension and an accident. Obviously, the application of Aristotelian categories and distinctions is insufficient to capture the role of the sign of historic episcopal succession, but Gerhard's reason for using the category of accidents is twofold. Historically, it is important to note that personal and local succession have not always and permanently been characteristics of the Church. From a theological perspective, Gerhard argues that persons and places cannot ensure the apostolicity of the church over time, but only the consensus on doctrine.[25] Gerhard does not rule out personal and

---

[24]   Since Bellarmine defined historic episcopal succession as a characteristic of the church, a nota ecclesia, Gerhard discusses the whole issue only briefly in his doctrine of ministry, but in greater detail in his ecclesiology. See Gerhard, Locus XXII, Cap. XI/5, 435–453.

[25]   See. Gerhard, Locus XXII, Cap. XI/5, 190, 435a: 'Personae aliae in aliorum locum subeuntes non faciunt successionem, sed perpetuus doctrinae consensus, qui fidei vinculo posteriores prioribus conjungit.' In order to justify this claim, Gerhard goes back to the patristic tradition and presents numerous quotations of the Church Fathers ranging from Irenaeus to Tertullian, Gregory of Nazianzus, Eusebius and Jerome to Chrysostom and Augustine which illustrate that the fathers never used local and personal succession alone as an argument, but combined it with succession in faith, doctrine and religion (cf. Locus XXII, Cap. XI/5, 193, 438b–440b). In a second step of his argumentation Gerhard explores whether historic episcopal ordination had been a continuous sign of apostolicity in the Roman Catholic Church. The result is that 'successionem papalem non solum esse interruptam, sed etiam turpiter deformatam' (Locus XXII, Cap. XI/5, 197, 447a.).

local succession as a sign of apostolicity, but he makes very clear that personal and local succession cannot guarantee the apostolic succession of ministers and the church as a whole. In comparison with Gerhard's view, the Porvoo Common Statement is less restrictive and more nuanced in stating that the 'use of the sign of the historic episcopal succession does *not by itself* guarantee the fidelity of a church to every aspect of the apostolic faith, life and mission.'[26] While Gerhard did not deny personal and local succession as an external element of apostolic succession, his goal in his context was to reject Bellarmine's concept of historic apostolic succession as a necessary *nota ecclesiae*. In the Porvoo Common Statement, the sign of historic episcopal succession is not a precondition for the recognition of the apostolicity of a church, because 'mutual acknowledgement of our churches and ministries is theologically prior to the use of the sign of the laying on of hands in the historic succession.'[27] The sign is not taken as a condition and guarantee for apostolicity, but rather as 'a permanent challenge to fidelity and to unity, a summons to witness to, and a commission to realise more fully, the permanent characteristics of the Church of the apostles.'[28]

At the Meissen-led symposium on ministry in July 2021, Professor John Barclay from Durham University described in a paper on the early expansion of Christianity the 'rhizome-model' and the 'arboreal model' as two models of the emergence of churches. In light of this distinction, Gerhard's interpretation of the patristic discussion could be understood as making a case for the rhizome-model which would allow for several roots of historic succession at different places. He elaborates that the Fathers did not claim that the episcopal succession from the apostles had been established *only* in the Roman Church and that *only* in the Roman church had the apostolic doctrine been preserved. According to Gerhard's reading of the Fathers, when referring to the episcopal succession, the Roman church wanted only to assert that the Roman church had gained special prominence and fame in the first centuries as the seat of the ruler, because of the presence of Peter and Paul, the many martyrs and the virtue and steadfastness of the first Roman bishops. Yet, the dominant position of the Roman church vis-à-vis the other churches as the root and 'arbour' of apostolic succession is questionable.

---

[26] Porvoo Common Statement, § 51.
[27] Porvoo Common Statement § 53.
[28] Porvoo Common Statement § 51.

Gerhard's doctrine of ministry, particularly his analysis of episcopal succession, is important not only because it offered the framework for a Lutheran theology of ministry, but also because the distinction between doctrinal succession and personal and local succession allows for legitimate diversity regarding the order of apostolic succession. On the one hand, in emphasizing the constitutive role of doctrinal succession, Gerhard's account offers the reason why and in what sense apostolic succession exists in Lutheran churches in Germany in spite of the interim time of presbyteral ordinations at the Reformation. On the other hand, the argument for the legitimacy of presbyteral succession does not rule out the role of personal and local succession in episcopacy as a sign of the apostolicity of the church, as well as its catholicity. As Dorothea Wendebourg argued in her contribution to the Theological Conference in Cheltenham in 2001, the sign of episcopal ordination is of special relevance for Lutherans:

> because its purpose is to see to it that the Gospel continues to be proclaimed as it had been. The catholic dimension of the ministry in time is expressed through the fact that it is performed by ministers who are themselves in office. It is also enhanced by this practice because those who are engaged in the proclamation of the Gospel bear a special responsibility for its continuity and have specific expertise. In other words, the bestowal of the ministry by ministers bears witness to and provides support for the church's continuity in the apostolic truth – without, however, being able to guarantee this continuity, as especially the time of the Reformation amply shows. If the one who ordains holds an episcopal office and, thus, represents the unity of the church above the local level in a special way, the catholic dimension of ordination becomes even more perceptible because in this case both aspects of the church's oneness at all times and in all places explicitly come together. It is, therefore, equally adequate and expressive to make ordination the prerogative of those who hold episcopal offices – while it is a matter of discretion to which episcopal level ordination should be linked. The same is true of the installation of a new pastor in a congregation, and it is especially true of the installation of bishops, since here the catholic dimension of the ministry is not only expressed through the act but is also an explicit part of the office bestowed.[29]

Due to this theological significance of the sign of episcopal ordination, Luther and Melanchthon wanted to preserve it. Yet, the use of the sign

---

[29]   Dorothea Wendebourg, 'The One Ministry of the One Church', 318–319.

cannot guarantee apostolic teaching, and in cases of emergency one can do without it. It is consequently possible for Lutheran churches who use the sign of historic apostolic succession to acknowledge churches that have not been using the sign if there is consensus on doctrinal apostolic succession, which was the situation for Lutheran churches on the way to the Porvoo Common Statement. In contrast to Lutheran churches in the Porvoo Communion, the EKD currently does not to use the sign of historic episcopal succession for several reasons. One reason lies in the history of Lutheran churches in Germany which lived without historic apostolic succession in the episcopate for several hundred years, while preserving doctrinal succession as well as the sign of episcopal ordination. Another reason is that Lutheran churches in the EKD are in communion with other Protestant churches in the EKD which have different practices of *episkopé*. Such a move would erode the existing ecumenical agreement and cohesion between churches. Moreover, if some churches resumed the sign of historic apostolic succession, it could easily be misinterpreted as a retroactive question about the previous authority of the ministry and about the ministries in non-episcopal churches. As mentioned at the beginning, the mutual respect for differences among the Protestant churches in Germany with their different territorial, political and cultural backgrounds has become part of the history and identity of the EKD as a communion and in each individual church.

5. Legitimate diversity and Lutheran identity

In his definition and analysis of the different dimensions of apostolic succession, Johann Gerhard developed the criteria to further Lutheran notions of apostolicity by combining the principle of the unity of ministry with a distinction and relation between doctrinal and personal and local succession. This distinction helped later Lutheran ecumenists to find differentiated consensus on conditions of apostolicity with other churches. The principle of the unity of ministry also allowed him to rethink the distinction between the threefold ministry of bishop, presbyter and deacon. In a detailed analysis of biblical teaching in the Old and New Testament, he demonstrates that both the service of the Word and the service of *diakonia* are fundamental to the church, yet in their distinctive character.[30] While

[30]   Cf. Gerhard, Locus XXIII, Cap. V/2, 204–247, 136b–164a.

a deacon promotes works of Christian love as a living witness of the Gospel of love, bishops and pastors are responsible for apostolic teaching on the regional and local level. Although the distinction between bishops and pastors is a distinction *iure humano*, it is useful and efficient to ensure the order and harmony in the church. Although Gerhard does not argue for a threefold ministry in hierarchical order, he would not regard the threefold ministry as a church dividing issue.

Gerhard was a premodern thinker in the age of confessionalization. His goal was to explain Christian doctrine in line with the apostolic tradition in the New Testament and the doctrinal consensus on the principles of Reformation, and his theological ambition was to renew the church through pure teaching in theological education. Against Bellarmine and Roman theologians on the one hand and different types of enthusiast on the other, he argued that the Lutheran church had adopted the principles of the Reformation in the best possible way and therefore was truly the church. The modern topic of identity and its visible expressions was not a question for him. In the age of modern ecumenism, however, the principles of a Lutheran doctrine of ministry which Gerhard developed in his ecclesiology in a polemic context, allowed Lutherans to develop pathways for ecumenical conversation with churches with different orders. The principles of *tota ecclesia*, of the character of ordained ministry, of the relation between doctrinal and personal and local succession and the sign of apostolic succession, all helped to define what is essential for apostolic succession and where legitimate diversity is possible. This legitimate diversity allows Lutheran churches worldwide to be in communion even though some of them use the sign of historic apostolic succession and have the threefold ministry in hierarchical order whereas others have the praxis of episcopal ordination, but no *historic* personal and local succession. Moreover, in their ecumenical relations Lutheran churches can recognize apostolic succession in churches with different orders when their ordained ministry and *episkopé* is ordered in a way to serve and ensure public proclamation of the Gospel in apostolic truth. In retrospect, one might say that in building on the theological insights of the Wittenberg Reformation it has become part of the identity of Lutheran churches to explore the scope for legitimate diversity in service to the apostolicity of the church.

Oversight

A view from underneath

Alexander Hughes

Introduction

I have been asked to say something about oversight from a practical perspective. My claim to be able to speak on this topic lies in the fact that I
have spent about twelve years serving on a bishop's senior staff: for 5
years from 2003 to 2008 I was chaplain to the Bishop of Portsmouth,
Kenneth Stevenson, which meant that I was his closest colleague, confidant
and observer; and since 2014 I have been Archdeacon of Cambridge in
the Diocese of Ely. As an archdeacon, I have considerable leadership responsibility for parts of diocesan life – for example, I run all appointment
processes for parish clergy in my area – though I do everything in close dialogue with my bishop. So, I suppose you could say that I have direct experience of episcopal oversight from just underneath. What follows is not
an essay but a few observations, which could probably come in any order
and is far from exhaustive.

Capacity

My first observation is about capacity. A colleague told me that one of the
clergy in Ely diocese had complained about never getting any attention
from the bishop or the archdeacon. I replied (as a joke): 'Tell so and so to
do something really stupid and I'll be round in 10 minutes.' My point is
that in some ways the Church of England lives with an *illusion* of oversight.
Despite frequent complaints that there are too many bishops and archdeacons and other senior clergy these days, the fact is that there are not
enough of us to meet the expectations of many of our people and churches.
There is an attention deficit, as senior clergy find themselves with limited

scope to choose what they do rather than simply react to external pressures. This has not changed a great deal in twenty years, in my experience. I do not remember anything of my interview with Bishop Kenneth, except one comment: 'You've got to have the right stomach for this job, because you'll spend 90% of your time on the worst 10% of the Church of England.' This was, and still is, an exaggeration; but there are days – sometimes weeks – when that is exactly how it feels. The Cappadocian bishops' ministry of *parrhesia* (righteous frankness) and *paramuthia* (consolation), to which Morwenna Ludlow draws attention, feels quite contemporary in this respect.

To return to my main point: the Ordinal expects bishops to 'know their people and be known by them,' but the truth is that bishops and their senior colleagues are often not very available, unless there is an emergency. This is bound to be a disappointment to the priest who wrote in response to a recent clergy wellbeing survey: 'I just want someone to notice what I'm doing'. The survey was confidential, so it is impossible to know what provoked this candid statement, but it speaks to me of a pastoral need among the clergy, and others, which is not being fully met. Like most working people these days, clergy feel themselves under a lot of pressure to perform and deliver results, and they look up to the hierarchy for support. I am sure my bishop would love to know his people and be known by them better; and I would like to be more generally available in my archdeaconry; but everyone is stretched and the urgent often eclipses the important. We are a very long way from the early days of the church, when the *episkopos* was a local figure, closely engaged in day-to-day church life on the ground and in frequent correspondence with junior clergy colleagues in the mode of a master craftsman and his apprentice. I am sure that my email correspondence on behalf of the bishops I have served would be very poor reading compared, say, with the letters of St Basil.

Diocesan structures & shared episcope

The picture of a somewhat remote and over-stretched bishop leads quite well into my next observation, which is about the development of the diocese and the sharing of episcopal oversight. A diocese was originally an area of Roman civil administration. The ecclesiastical diocese emerged in the Constantinian era as a way to realise and manage the connection between bishops and their increasingly dispersed congregations. Significant parts of the bishop's presidency and oversight were imparted to priest-presbyters, expressed today in the idea of a shared 'cure of souls'.

After twenty centuries, the spread of the church and the growing complexity of ecclesiastical life now mean that we have long outgrown the kind of direct oversight bishops once exercised towards local congregations. Diocesan structures have evolved to mediate the bishop's responsibilities. There are diocesan boards of mission and ministry, and education, and social responsibility and so on, each with their own officer or director and a team of specialist staff. There is nothing sacrosanct about any of these mediating diocesan structures – you won't find anything about them in works of classical ecclesiology – yet they seem essential to maintaining the life of the church as it currently is. Archdeacons might fit into this category too. Therefore, although the diocese subsists in the relationship of local churches overseen by their bishop, reality demands that the bishop shares oversight with a range of others.

For example, the Ordinal charges the bishop to 'discern and foster the gifts of the Spirit in all who follow Christ, commissioning them to minister in his name'. In practice, however, this work is devolved first to parish clergy and other local people, to discern gifts of ministry among themselves; then to the diocesan vocations team – an array of chaplains and advisers, usually overseen by a Diocesan Director of Ordinands – who pass some people on to the National Ministry Team responsible for selecting candidates for ordination training; and then on to various Theological Education Institutions and eventually to a local training incumbent. In theory, the bishop can intervene at any point, but it is not realistic to imagine this will happen very often or very effectively. Discerning, nurturing and deploying vocations is necessarily a time-consuming business and involves a degree of expertise, which most bishops simply do not have. I can speak from my experience as a bishop's chaplain here, since Kenneth Stevenson was one of the few bishops who ever overturned the recommendation of a national advisory panel not to send someone for ordination training. In the one instance I can remember clearly, the bishop came to regret his decision.

It is simply not possible these days for the bishop to oversee selection and formation for ministry without delegating almost all of the work to others to the point where, in effect, the bishop's ministry as described in the Ordinal is in fact a corporate responsibility. The distribution of the bishop's role in this, and other fields, significantly attenuates the meaning of her or his personal oversight. In practice, episcopé is a dispersed and corporate responsibility and activity, which often operates at some distance from the *episkopos*. When people and parishes look for support from above (so to speak), the bishop is unlikely to be their first port of call. And the decreasing number of stipendiary clergy in some areas means that more and more parish clergy are overseeing teams of other junior clergy and lay ministers, in a pattern that might look a lot like the work of a primitive *episkopos*.

There is another point about the modern diocese I would like to make. From an ecclesiological point of view, the diocese may be understood to subsist in the relationship between local churches overseen by the bishop, but that does not present the complete picture. In 1925, Diocesan Boards of Finance were established as incorporated charitable companies. In other words, a Church of England diocese now exists as a legal entity in its own right, and with that status comes a wide range of duties and responsibilities, which intrude (for better or worse) upon the bishop's ministry of oversight. The law and the Charity Commission treat a diocese like a kind of business, which affects the position of the bishop. On one hand, the bishop is widely perceived as the 'boss' at the head of the organisation. On the other hand, the bishop may be marginalised in many internal processes, partly because much of the diocese's business is overseen and conducted by others and also because the bishop is probably not competent to meet the diocese's statutory and other responsibilities, of which there is no mention in the Ordinal or textbooks on ecclesiology. I remember Bishop Kenneth telling me once that he had no interest in running the Church of England in that sense.

The bishop may be the head of the organisation, but she or he is not in a position to run it effectively, or compliantly – or even safely. I use this last word advisedly, because the recent advance in Safeguarding awareness and procedures has exposed a regrettable clash between some bishops' instinctive or inherited pastoral and institutional responses and the demands of process-driven management and leadership behaviour. Expectations about the exercise of oversight are being imposed in new ways, and bishops, among others, are having to catch up and adapt, or face serious consequences. There is a discernible shift to increase the accountability of bishops and reduce the deference with which they are treated. In some quarters their credibility is seriously undermined.

I might add that the Covid-19 pandemic has also had an impact in this respect, as some people have expressed frustration at the way in which the church's leaders have acquiesced in the restriction of religious freedoms. The same erosion of episcopal authority can be seen in ongoing disagreements about gender and sexuality, in which some bishops are accused (by some) of undermining, rather than upholding and proclaiming, the faith of the church. It is very hard for a bishop to inhabit her or his role as symbol of church unity in a world of clashing identities and longstanding disputes.

I want to move now to quite a different topic, which may be said to incorporate various elements of the episcopal task as set out in the Ordinal, though couched in very different terms. The Ordinal speaks of leading, shepherding, nurturing, feeding, serving, caring, discerning, commissioning and building up the Body of Christ, all of which echo the words of scripture. The contemporary Church of England talks quite a lot about strategy and often construes leadership in that light. Furthermore, the focus of the Ordinal is on holiness, justice, righteousness, peace, and the gospel, whereas many bishops in the Church of England today are greatly preoccupied with institutional survival.

Though dioceses are largely autonomous entities, they are bound to the National Church by various systems, not least the in- and out-flow of funds. In order to win bids for national funding, dioceses have to demonstrate their strategic purposes; so, in the scramble for resources, every diocese now has to have a strategy. The rise of diocesan strategy is not only due to financial accountability to the National Church; it is also about local stewardship of resources. The rising cost of running a diocese and the dwindling size of congregations mean that we can no longer afford all of our inherited expectations about deployment of clergy and the provision of worship; and the experience of decline has inevitably raised questions about the efficacy of our inherited ways of doing things. These are existential crises of different but related kinds, and people naturally look to bishops to address them. So, we have learnt about vision and strategy, mainly by observing how other organisations do it.

The problem is that you cannot strategize the Church of England in the same way as other organisations. Take the Ely diocesan strategy for example (for which I am partly responsible). I do not intend to go into the details of its content; rather what matters is the mechanism. Our strategy comprises five 'levers for change'. The image was taken from a picture of an old-fashioned railway signal box, in which someone pulled levers that moved tracks in order to direct the passage of trains. It's a nice image, I think, but the problem with the levers of our diocesan strategy is that they are not securely attached to anything, so you can pull on them as hard as you like at the top, but there is no guarantee that anything will move at the bottom.

Historical checks and balances between episcopal leadership, synodical governance and parish and clergy autonomy, within a largely voluntary body, mean that nothing can be imposed 'from above' and implementation is only by consent. This does not mean that nothing can be done, but it highlights that the work of leading change involves presiding over a scattered and not fully coherent range of stakeholders and gatekeepers (to use the jargon), who may respond with varying degrees of acceptance or resistance. The 'head' of the institutional 'body' may set various priorities, but the sub-systems and micro-organisations within the body are largely free to decide for themselves. This has given rise to the occasional quip that in theory the Church of England is episcopally led and synodically governed, though in practice it is synodically stymied and episcopally frustrated. The bishop and other senior clergy have little more than the power of 'good speech' to inspire, motivate and encourage those whom they lead; and the weight of their speech depends on the residue of institutional deference and popular approval. And there is no possibility that a modern Church of England bishop could stack the odds in her or his favour through making favourable appointments, as the Cappadocians did with their episcopal college, since parishes have an absolute veto in such matters.

Apostolic ministry

I set out above some of the key phrases from the Ordinal denoting the ministry of bishops, which were largely focused on building up the church in various ways. There are other phrases – 'speaking in the name of God ... expounding the gospel of salvation ... following the example of the prophets and the teaching of the apostles ... proclaim[ing] the gospel boldly' – which link to the view that an important part of the bishop's role is to defend and declare the faith of the church (regardless of whether there is understood to be an essential ecclesiological link between the bearers of the apostolic tradition and the heirs of an apostolic succession).

Throughout the church's history there have been some fine bishop-theologians. People will disagree about the extent to which an educated gift for theology is a requirement for episcopal office in the Church of England today, but it seems that expectations (and the necessary allowances in terms of time and opportunity for study) are not high. My former Bishop Kenneth was unusual in managing to pursue his academic interests alongside his ministry; though in this he benefitted from overseeing a small diocese with a supportive and capable team, whom he trusted to run the diocese. By contrast, the prominent New Testament scholar Tom Wright found it impossible to combine his 'continuing vocation to be a writer, teacher and broadcaster ... with the complex demands and duties of a diocesan bishop' and therefore resigned as Bishop of Durham.[1]

In this regard, bishops' experience is similar to that of parochial and other clergy, for whom the general demands of ministry leave little or no time for study. It is a concern for bishops, though, whose high profile gives particular opportunities for the distinctly apostolic ministry of evangelism. It is a long time since Friedrich Schleiermacher saw that the church in Western Europe was surrounded by the 'cultured despisers' of religion, but not so long since Rowan Williams began his archiepiscopate with a longing 'that the years to come will see Christianity in this country able to capture the imagination of our culture'.[2] As prominent local and national leaders, bishops need time and resources to help them think, in order to engage and help others to engage with the world in the third Christian millennium. There are some (inside and outside the church) who say they have looked in vain to the bishops to know what the Christian faith has to say about a global pandemic, for example. This may be undeserved, and on the basis of my experience it is likely that bishops have been addressing the question frequently through their preaching ministry; but perceptions are what they are. The wider point is that Church of England bishops have lately been provided with much-needed support for their management functions – the so-called 'Mini MBAs'[3] – but do not always seem to be resourced in other ways, which link more directly with their apostolic calling.

Of course, it is also true that the theological environment today is quite contested, which makes it harder for bishops to unite people around an agreed teaching of the faith – at least, not in certain areas. The strength of feeling and belief on different sides of some arguments also makes it difficult for some bishops to speak openly about their own theological conclusions, lest they alienate one or other group under their oversight. The Church of England has attempted to address this structurally over the issue of the ordination of women, by the innovation of Provincial Episcopal Visitors to cater for different theological views (either Anglo-Catholic or

[1]   'Bishop of Durham to Leave Diocese' *Thinking Anglicans* (27 April 2010) at: https://www.thinkinganglicans.org.uk/4335-2/ (accessed 4 January 2022).

[2]   'Church must capture the imagination', *BBC News* (23 July, 2002) at: http://news.bbc.co.uk/1/hi/uk/2146359.stm (accessed 04.01.22).

[3]   'Go forth and MBA, Welby tells bishops', *The Times* (11 January 2015) <https://www.thetimes.co.uk/article/go-forth-and-mba-welby-tells-bishops-jsw9v6x6bx2> [accessed 04.01.22].

Evangelical-Complementarian). This may have been the best, or only, solution to overcome that particular impasse; but it highlights the difficulty of shepherding when the flock has divided and fenced itself into different fields.

Conclusion

In my experience, then, there are a number of strands informing the practice of episcopé. There is the ecclesiological strand: the hallowed phrases of the Ordinal and the textbook accounts of what makes the church 'The Church'. Then there are the multiple minds of church people, who expect episcopacy to meet their particular wants and needs, which are neither singular nor uncontested. And then there is the constraint placed upon bishops by the nature of institutional church life. I remember Bishop Kenneth used to say to me that he tried to do some of what he *had* to, some of what he *ought* to and some of what he *wanted* to – though I would observe that his three-legged stool was very unstable. Perhaps a more positive way to say this is that the exercise of episcopé has proved to be very flexible and adaptable, with different elements coming to the fore or receding, depending on circumstances. What is not always clear is whether the practice is being driven by principle or pragmatism.

Identity and Episcopé

An EKD Perspective in Ecumenical Horizon

Miriam Haar

1. Introduction

'How does your Church's perception of its identity affect its understanding of the significance of *episcopé,* including in its relations with other churches?' This is the question that was posed to the participants of the Meissen-led Colloquium on episcopé (5–6 July 2021). As the aim of the colloquium was to find out to what extent the understanding of one's own ecclesial identity influences the understanding of episcopé and the relations with other churches, the starting point of this paper was to contribute to this purpose from the perspective of the Evangelical Church in Germany (EKD).[1]

According to the theme of the colloquium, the first step to answer this question would be to explore the identity of the EKD. In a second step, one would examine how this perception of identity affects the EKD's understanding of the significance of episcopé and its relations with other churches. Yet, the discussion at the colloquium has shown that these two steps are deeply interrelated and that they cannot be separated easily. As a consequence, this paper explores the themes of identity and episcopé in relation to the EKD not as two completely separate steps, but as interrelated aspects.

Since any attempt to give a full account of the EKD's identity would go beyond the scope of this paper, I offer a few reflections on the perception

---

[1]   As this paper was presented as a short input for discussion at the Meissen-led Colloquium before the Theological Conference, it has a different character, style and focus from the presentations at the Theological Conference. It was revised for publication in light of the discussion during the colloquium, but the original intention of the paper is still clear.

of the EKD's identity to the extent that they are relevant for the understanding of episcopé and for ecumenical relations.

2. Aspects of the EKD's Identity

2.1. Ecclesial Identity – Identities

It is not an easy task to know where to find the identity of a given church. When exploring the perception of the EKD's identity, one might debate about which approach should be taken as the identity of a church is formed through complex processes. Different influences, such as doctrinal or liturgical, play a role in forming the identity of a church. Various narratives, historical, sociological, and political also feature in these processes.[2] Where is the identity of the EKD to be located? Where is it expressed? Is the 'EKD' perceived as an institution, a communion of *Landeskirchen* (regional churches) or as *communio* of believers? These are but a few questions to be explored.

Although there is a distinction to be made between individual and group identity, the core of our identity, both personally and as a church, is in God; it is received from God. The identity of a church is most clearly expressed in its liturgy (including hymnody), structure, and mission. Hymns have a powerful influence in shaping identity both of individual believers and of the church as a whole. At the same time the mission of the church is a basic identity marker of her identity. The mission of the Church yields the commission of Christians to *leiturgia* (worship), *martyria* (witness), *diakonia* (service) and *koinonia* (life in community). Yet, there are also other perceptions of a church's identity. Doctrinally, the identity is rooted in the Holy Scriptures. Ecumenically, the identity is defined by her confession(s). Politically, a church's identity is submitted to various tensions and interests in the society. Culturally, it is influenced by history and social class. These different aspects show that identity is neither static nor fixed, but in flux and constantly developing.

---

[2]   See, for example, the lecture of Sr. PD Dr Nicole Grochowina on the role of (historic) narratives in the formation of Protestant Identity at the Digital Academy of the Evangelischer Bund Hessen on 27 January 2022 at: https://junge-theo logie. de/6-lecture/?fbclid=IwAR2BiHcYjedb91snfU-ogQlFSiWSzIQ-W2bQGUn5CKkF7 tk1bk9eViyArQc (accessed 10 February 2022).

Despite the limitations of this paper, a historical and doctrinal approach to identity has been chosen as the perception of the EKD's identity is explored for the sake of the discussion of episcopé and not, for example, regarding ecumenical spirituality.[3]

2.2. Aspects of Historical and Organisational Identity: The Development of the EKD from a 'Kirchenbund' to a 'Church'

In 1948 the EKD was founded as a church federation (*Kirchenbund*) of Germany's Lutheran, Reformed and United churches, to further deepen their sense of fellowship – after the shared experience of the 'church struggle' (*Kirchenkampf*) during the Nazi period from 1933 – and to constitute joint representation of the regional churches.[4] Due to the different confessional status (*Bekenntnisstand*) of its member churches, the EKD initially constituted itself as a church federation after the Second World War without pulpit and altar fellowship. Nevertheless, it was to be a church and make the 'existing fellowship' visible. As a joint federation of Lutheran, Reformed and United member churches, the EKD was without an ecclesial quality of its own.

With the adoption of the *Leuenberg Agreement* in 1973, full pulpit and altar fellowship was achieved among all the regional churches, and

---

[3]   As the purpose of this paper was to contribute to the Meissen-led Colloquium on Episcopé, literature on the debates on identity such as Stephen Sykes, *The Identity of Christianity: Theologians and the Essence of Christianity from Schleiermacher to Barth* (Minneapolis, MN: Fortress Press, 1984) is not included here. For explorations of confessional identities such as Lutheran Identity, see for example Theodor Dieter (ed.), *Lutherische Identität / Lutheran Identity*, Im Auftrag des Instituts für Ökumenische Forschung in Straßburg herausgegeben von Theodor Dieter / Edited on behalf of the Institute for Ecumenical Research in Strasbourg by Theodor Dieter (Leipzig: Evangelische Verlagsanstalt, 2019), or the study process on 'Lutheran Identity' of the Lutheran World Federation: https://www.lutheranworld.org/content/lutheran-identities-study-process (accessed 10 February 2022). For Reformed identity, see, for example, Margit Ernst-Habib, *Reformierte Identität weltweit. Eine Interpretation neuerer Bekenntnisse aus der reformierten Tradition*, FSÖTh 158 (Göttingen: Vandenhoeck&Ruprecht, 2017).

[4]   On this see: https://www.ekd.de/geschichte-evangelische-kirche-deutschland-57759.htm (accessed 10 February 2022); Oliver Schuegraf and Florian Hübner, *Lutheran – Reformed – United. A Pocket Guide to the Denominational Landscape in Germany* (Hannover: German National Committee of the Lutheran World Federation, 2017), 36–37; Wolf-Dieter Hauschild, 'Evangelische Kirche in Deutschland (EKD),' *RGG*[4] 2 (1999), 1713–1721.

thus the EKD was also understood as a church fellowship.[5] As a consequence, in 1983, an amendment to the Basic Constitution was passed which established church fellowship, i.e. pulpit and altar fellowship.

While attempts at reform from the 1970s towards a 'federal church' were not successful, there was a rapprochement to this goal in 1991 when the EKD and the Federation of Protestant Churches in the GDR (*Bund Evangelischer Kirchen in der DDR*) merged. The reorientation of the EKD as church, which required the approval of the member churches and which sparked debate about the preservation of Lutheran identity, was decided by the EKD Synod in 2015. Article 1 of the Basic Constitution of the EKD states:

> The Evangelical Church in Germany is a communion of its Lutheran, Reformed and United member churches. It understands itself to be part of the one Church of Jesus Christ. It respects the confessional foundations of the member churches and congregations and presupposes that they put their confession into effect in the teachings, life and order of their churches. Church fellowship exists between the member churches pursuant to the Agreement of Reformation Churches in Europe [i.e. the Leuenberg Agreement].[6]

This statement defining the EKD emphasises more strongly the ecclesiological and ecumenical significance of the EKD. Although today the EKD is a communion of 20 Lutheran, Reformed, and United Protestant Churches, each member church still has a distinctive character shaped by its particular confessional tradition. Each is constrained to a particular region and puts the emphasis on local parish life.[7]

This short summary of the EKD's history illustrates that the development of its identity was not accidental, and that its identity evolved over

---

[5] *Agreement between Reformation Church in Europe (Leuenberg Agreement) 1973, Trilingual edition with an introduction (bilingual), By order of the Executive Committee for the Leuenberg Doctrinal Conversations* (Frankfurt am Main: Verlag Otto Lembeck, 1993). The text of 1973 arose from a very complex process which included, for example, the "Arnoldshain Theses on Holy Communion" (1957) and the "Theses on Church Fellowship" (1970) (See Martin Friedrich, *Von Marburg bis Leuenberg: der lutherisch-reformierte Gegensatz und seine Überwindung*, Walltrop: Spener, 1999).

[6] Art. 1 (1 and 2) GO EKD: Grundordnung der Evangelischen Kirche in Deutschland at: https://www.kirchenrecht-ekd.de/document/3435 (accessed 3 January 2022).

[7] See, for example, https://www.ekd.de/ekd_en/ds_doc/facts_and_figures_2016. pdf (accessed 3 January 2022).

time between the poles of continuity and change. The identity of the EKD is a result of a history larger than its own. Different stages in the development of the EKD's identity need to be seen in their distinctive historic context. As the EKD's perception of its identity is influenced by historical developments, these developments and debates show the influence of non-doctrinal factors on the development of ecclesial identity.

2.3. Aspects of Doctrinal Identity:
The Ecclesiological Self-Understanding of the EKD

A crucial element of the ecclesiological self-understanding of the EKD is found in Article 1 of its Basic Constitution: the EKD respects the different confessional foundations (*Bekenntnisgrundlagen*) of its member churches. An indispensable prerequisite for the recognition of the confessional traditions of its member churches is that the EKD does not give itself a confession. In other words, the EKD can only adequately safeguard the recognition of the confessional churches (*Konfessionskirchen*) as member churches by respecting their confessional traditions, and it does so by not giving itself a particular confession and by not privileging any particular confession.[8] Yet, it is not the case that the EKD is entirely without a confessional foundation. On the contrary, in a theologically well-balanced way, the EKD's constitution names the foundations of its self-understanding as a church: namely, the Gospel, the confessions of the early church, the *Barmen Theological Declaration* and the *Leuenberg Agreement*. The EKD's constitution also states the importance of the confessions of the Reformation, emphasizing that it respects them and grants them their hermeneutical function for the understanding of Scripture and the confessions of the early church in the member churches.[9] Accordingly, the central ecclesiological function of the EKD is to maintain and manifest the unity of its member churches while recognising and fostering the confessional diversity that has developed.[10]

---

[8] See Christine Axt-Piscalar, 'Zur ekklesiologischen Bedeutung der EKD und der VELKD vor dem Hintergrund der Frage nach der Bekenntnisgrundlage der EKD und der Weiterentwicklung des „Verbindungsmodells"', Impulsreferat für die Generalsynode der VELKD in Düsseldorf 2013, para. 3 at: https://www.velkd.de/downloads/131108_DS07b_Impulspapier_Verbindungsmodell_Axt-Piscalar.pdf (accessed 2 July 2021).

[9] Ibid., para. 3.

[10] Ibid., para. 1; 4.

To comprehend this ecclesiological self-understanding better, it is important to look at the recent ecclesiological developments within the EKD. The so-called *Verbindungsmodell* ('connection or liaison model') which had already come into effect on 1 January 2007 aims at strengthening the co-operation of the confessional church federations, the United Evangelical Lutheran Church in Germany (*Vereinigte Evangelisch-Lutherische Kirche in Deutschland / VELKD*) and the Union of Evangelical Churches in the EKD (*Union Evangelischer Kirchen in der EKD/UEK*) within the EKD. These developments aim at expressing a shared Protestant identity and have fostered closer cooperation between these two bodies under the umbrella of the EKD.[11] Since 2009, the assemblies of the Lutheran and United churches as well as the EKD Synod have been meeting at the same place, around the same time and with the corresponding staff. All three church administrative offices are in Hanover, and the UEK has already been largely integrated into the EKD.

In 2015, the EKD Synod in Bremen passed an amendment to its constitution, according to which the EKD as a communion of the 20 Protestant regional churches also became a church in the theological sense. The EKD is church as a 'communion of its member churches.' This is the formula that found approval after years of debate about the EKD's ecclesial status. In other words, the EKD is itself a church as the *communio* of its member churches, as it realises the representation of the unity of its member churches.[12]

The process that led to the decision of the EKD Synod in 2015 which defined the self-understanding of the EKD as a church required the approval of the member churches. These developments sparked a debate about maintaining Lutheran identity.[13] It is crucial, though often forgotten, that these sorts of developments and debates show the influence of non-doctrinal factors on the development of ecclesial identity.

---

[11] At: https://www.ekd.de/Gliedkirchliche-Zusammenschluesse-EKD-14049.htm (accessed 2 July 2021).

[12] See Axt-Piscalar, 'Zur ekklesiologischen Bedeutung der EKD und der VELKD', para. 4.

[13] The VELKD 'wird für die Pflege lutherischer Identität Sorge tragen. Dass damit keine Abgrenzungsstrategien verbunden sind, sondern das Ganze von der Einsicht lebt, dass auch das Andere als eine evangeliumsgemäße Ausgestaltung von Kirche anerkannt wird und im Spiegel des Anderen das Eigene wiederum noch bewusster erfasst wird' (Axt-Piscalar, 'Zur ekklesiologischen Bedeutung der EKD und der VELKD', para. 6).

The General Synod of the VELKD and the General Conference of the UEK had already approved the agreements on the *Verbindungsmodell* at their meetings in Bonn. In November 2017, the EKD Synod voted on the agreement that included a joint church administrative office of EKD, UEK and VELKD.[14] The contract states that '[t]he identity-forming significance of the fields of ecumenism and partnership work, theology and liturgy will be taken into account.'[15] On 1 January 2018, the joint church office in Hanover began its work in the new structures. This means that today the VELKD und UEK are united under the umbrella of the EKD.

The EKD's *Verbindungsmodell* has only been possible because of Leuenberg, as the adoption of the *Leuenberg Agreement* enabled full pulpit and table fellowship among all Regional Churches and an understanding of the EKD as a communion of churches. This was possible because for the EKD, the main ecumenical frame of reference is the Community of Protestant Churches in Europe (CPCE).[16] At the same time, the Lutherans in the EKD emphasized that the basic model for unity for them was not Porvoo, but the *Leuenberg Modell* which is expressed, for example, in the CPCE Study 'Ministry, Ordination, Episkopé and Theological Education' of 2020. It states that the unity of the church in the Protestant understanding can only be realised as a unity in reconciled diversity.[17] It expresses the conviction that, according to the Protestant understanding, the visible unity of the church worldwide will be a differentiated unity.[18] Thus, by standing on the ground of the *Leuenberg Agreement* and by implementing its insight – church fellowship in reconciled diversity – in its basic constitution, it was possible for the EKD to define its identity positively, and to avoid defining itself principally in terms of oppo-

---

[14]   See Schuegraf and Hübner, *Lutheran – Reformed – United*, 30–37.
[15]   https://www.ekd.de/Gliedkirchliche-Zusammenschluesse-EKD-14049.htm (accessed 2 July 2021).
[16]   This development points to ways in which ecumenical encounters make an impact on confessional identity. A deeper analysis would go beyond the scope of this paper. But see Silke Dangel, *Konfessionelle Identität und ökumenische Prozesse. Analysen zum interkonfessionellen Diskurs des Christentums*, TBT 168 (Berlin/ Boston: de Gruyter, 2014).
[17]   See Mario Fischer and Martin Friedrich (eds), *Ministry, ordination, episkopé and theological education*, Leuenberg Documents 13 (Leipzig: Evangelische Verlagsanstalt GmbH, ²2020), 23 ff.
        https://www.eva-leipzig.de/product_info.php?info=p5046_Amt—Ordination—Episkop—und-theologische-Ausbildung—-Ministry—ordination—episkop—and-theological-education.html (accessed 21 March 2022).
[18]   See ibid., 37.

sition towards another church tradition, namely the Roman Catholic Church.

The understanding of ecclesial identity which is expressed in the *Verbindungsmodell* is closely linked to the EKD's understanding of the unity of the church as 'unity in reconciled diversity'[19] as it gives room to the Lutheran, Reformed and United confessions while still uniting the churches of different confessional status into *one* church. This understanding of unity as '*Einheit unter Anerkennung der gestalteten Vielfalt*', a unity that exists while recognizing the diversity that is being shaped, is crucial for the identity of the EKD.[20]

The understanding of unity is not only crucial for the understanding of ecclesial identity, it also has implications for the understanding and significance of episcopé. In this regard, the CPCE study 'Ministry, ordination, episkopé and theological education' expresses a crucial insight in para. 22, where it acknowledges that a 'hermeneutics of unity in reconciled diversity is not of course sufficient in itself to overcome church divisions which are evident in an ecumenical context, particularly over the question of ministries', and stresses that '[c]hurch divisions are not simply the result of historical developments but are also the consequence of decisions taken by the churches and their leaders'. It emphasizes that '[a] dynamic view of confessional identity reckons with the activity of the Holy Spirit, and that also means accepting the historical developments of identities.'[21] These developments show the doctrinal side of the development of the EKD from a mere federation to a church. They illustrate that like personal identity, ecclesial identity is not a static quality, but develops. This means that a dynamic view of ecclesial identity is needed.

3. The Understanding and Significance of Episcopé

After trying to outline different aspects of the EKD's identity, I now ask how this perception of its identity affects the EKD's understanding of the significance of *episcopé*, including in its relationship with other churches.

---

19 *Kirchengemeinschaft nach evangelischem Verständnis. Ein Votum zum geordneten Miteinander bekenntnisverschiedener Kirchen*, EKD Texte 69, Hannover 2001 at: https://www.ekd.de/22764.htm (accessed 2 July 2021).

20 See Axt-Piscalar, 'Zur ekklesiologischen Bedeutung der EKD und der VELKD', para. 1.

21 See *Ministry, ordination, episkopé and theological education*, 37.

3.1. Elements of Church Leadership in the 'Landeskirchen'

As the EKD is the communion of twenty Regional Churches, it is necessary to look at the structures of church leadership and the diverse expressions of episcopé in the Regional Churches (*landeskirchliche Leitung*).[22] There are four different elements of church leadership in the Regional Churches.[23] They all exercise episcopé together. (1) The episcopal component is exercised by the bishop (or church president or *praeses* depending on the regional church), the deputy bishop (*vice-praeses* etc.), and regional bishops (prelate etc.). Their tasks include spiritual leadership, ordination, and visitation. (2) The synodal component is exercised by the elected, appointed, or hereditary members of the synod. The synod oversees legislation, budget, and election of leadership staff. (3) The consistorial (*Konsistorial*) component is the governing body and the administrative office (*Kollegium und Verwaltungsbehörde*). The consistories emerged during the Reformation period. They governed the church on behalf of the *Landesherr* (sovereign) and were staffed collegially with various professional groups. They were permanent administrative offices. When the regional church regiment (*Landesherrliches Kirchenregiment*) was abolished in 1918, these administrative offices remained and formed a factor of stability. Members of other governing bodies form the church governance (*Kirchenleitung*) by virtue of office or election. They are responsible for the integration of the church leadership, for norm-setting and for staff decisions.

Three different 'models' can be distinguished with regard to the relationship between these four elements of church leadership in the Regional Churches. (1) The so-called *Einheitsmodell* ('Model of Unity') is, for example, exercised in the Evangelical Church in the Rhineland;[24] (2) the *Trennungsmodell* ('Model of Separation'), for example, in the Evangelical-

---

[22] For the different legal frameworks regarding church leadership and church governance structures in various Regional Churches, see, for example: Bavaria: Art. 41–71 Kirchenverfassung (https://landeskirche.bayern-evangelisch.de/downloads/ELKB_Kirchenverfassung_Stand_2020.pdf); Baden: Art. 64–86 Grundordnung (https://kirchenrecht-baden.de/document/27489); Palatinate: Art. 65-100a Verfassung (https://www.kirchenrecht-evpfalz.de/document/14452); Hannover: Art. 43–60 Kirchenverfassung (https://kirchenrecht-evlka.de/document/44991) (all accessed 1 December 2021).

[23] See also Bernd Oberdorfer's paper in this volume.

[24] See Art. 128–162 KO (https://www.kirchenrecht-ekir.de/) (accessed 1 December 2021).

Lutheran Church in Bavaria;[25] and (3) the *Gemischter Typ* ('Mixed Model'), for example, in the Evangelical Church in Kurhessen-Waldeck.[26] The historical reasons for the formation of these church governance structures go back to the Reformation and its aftermath. These include overcoming the difference between clergy and laity, distinguishing between spiritual and legal leadership, elements of regional church leadership (*landeskirchlicher Leitung*) that include visitations, consistories, superintendents, and church ordinances (*Kirchenordnungen*) and the emergence of the regional church regiment.

During the period of enlightenment collegiality became more of a focus. In the nineteenth century the loss of confessional homogeneity led to pluralisation. Developments in the nineteenth century also led to the separation of state and church, of parish and municipality, as well as to presbyterial and synodal ordinances (*Ordnungen*). Parallel to the growth of parliaments in the states, synods were introduced. When the regional church regiment had come to an end in 1918, the enactment of church constitutions followed. When after the establishment of the 'Reich Church' (*Reichskirche*) and during the *Kirchenkampf* ('church struggle') the Theological Declaration of Barmen was issued in 1934, it connected the message and the order of the Church, especially in its theses III and IV. After 1945 fundamental discussions on church leadership took place and constitutional revisions followed.[27]

3.2. Structures of Church Leadership in the EKD

At the EKD level episcopé is exercised through the EKD synod, the Council and the Church Conference. The EKD's highest governing body is its annual synod, which can adopt church legislation and issue formal declarations. The leading clergy and legal experts of the member churches meet in the Church Conference to deliberate on the common concerns of the member churches. The two bodies elect the 15-person Council that directs, manages and represents the EKD. The chairperson of the Council, who is always one of the leading clergy of one of the regional churches, represents

---

25 See Art. 41–71 KVerf. (https://landeskirche.bayern-evangelisch.de/downloads/ELKB_Kirchenverfassung_Stand_2020.pdf) (accessed 1 December 2021).
26 See Art. 89–141 GO (https://www.kirchenrecht-ekkw.de/) (all accessed 1 December 2021).
27 See the work of Johannes Heckel (1889–1963), Erik Wolf (1902–1977) or Hans Dombois (1907–1997).

the EKD in the public sphere. In other words, there are four dimensions of church governance in the EKD: episcopal (in the wider sense of a personal leadership through a leading clergyperson), synodal, consistorial and collegial. To be more precise, the episcopal, synodal and consistorial are held together in collegial bodies of governance. Accordingly, what is expressed in the study 'Lutheran Identity – Lutherische Identität' of the LWF's Institute for Ecumenical Studies in Strasbourg also applies to EKD and its member churches. The study claims that the

> supra-regional ministers have taken different forms according to their time and place. In this way structures developed in which the responsibility for supra-regional direction and oversight was exercised in a personal manner (by bishops or church presidents), in a collegial manner (by cooperation among church leaders or the conference of bishops), and in a synodical manner (by synod gatherings including non-ordained persons). Episcopé is not always exercised solely by an episkopos (that is, a bishop) but through the interaction of different persons and institutions in charge of the direction of the church.'[28]

4. Identity, Episcopé and Ecumenical Relations

The convergence document *Baptism, Eucharist and Ministry (BEM)* (1982)[29] of the Faith and Order Commission of the World Council of Churches states in the second section of its discussion of 'Ministry'[30] that, first and foremost, ordained ministry should be exercised in three different forms, in 'a personal, collegial and communal way'[31]. The re-

---

[28] See Dieter (ed.), *Lutheran Identity*, 34.
[29] *Baptism, Eucharist and Ministry*, Faith and Order Paper 111 (Geneva: World Council of Churches, 1982).
[30] 'Guiding Principles for the Exercise of the Ordained Ministry in the Church' (Ibid., para. M 26f.) (III B).
[31] Ibid., para. M 26. *BEM* says that the 'ordained ministry should be exercised in a personal, collegial and communal way'. The commentary (26) reminds the churches that in some churches one of these three dimensions of ordained ministry has been over-emphasized at the expense of another, but that these three dimensions need to be kept together. Although *BEM* is based on earlier achievements of bilateral and multilateral agreement, it rarely refers explicitly back to those documents. It is only in the Commentary (26) that it builds explicitly on a recommendation which was made at the First World Conference on Faith and Order at Lau-

sponses to *BEM* seem to agree tacitly on *BEM*'s definition of episcopé as 'supervising [the community's] life'[32], but discuss the exercise of ordained ministry in personal, collegial and communal ways in great detail.

The EKD's understanding of episcopé is in agreement with *BEM* regarding the basic understanding of the exercise of episcopé in so far as episcopé is exercised in personal, communal and collegial ways. *BEM* understood episcopé mainly as a function of the episcopate. For the EKD episcopé is not only part of the tasks of the episcopate but takes place on different levels as in the EKD ecclesial governance and shared oversight are practised on various levels of the church. The element of episcopé is embedded in the personal, collegial and communal.

BEM's distinction of 'personal, collegial, and communal' can be found in many ecumenical dialogues on episcopé, in multilateral documents such as *The Church. Towards a Common Vision*,[33] as well as in bilateral dialogues. Both the *Meissen Agreement* (1988)[34] and the *Porvoo Statement* (1996)[35] repeat verbatim the following sentence from the Anglican-Lutheran *Niagara Report* (1987), although the *Meissen Agreement* does not mention the *Niagara Report* by name: 'We believe that a ministry of pastoral oversight (episcopé), exercised in personal, collegial and communal ways is necessary as witness to and safeguard of the unity and apostolicity of the Church.'[36] The *Reuilly Declaration* (2001) similarly includes this same phrase in its acknowledgements.[37]

---

sanne in 1927 and calls for an 'appropriate place [for episcopal, presbyteral and congregational systems] in the order of life of a reunited Church' (ibid., para. M 26 Commentary).

[32] *BEM*, para. M 14 Commentary.

[33] *The Church. Towards a Common Vision*, Faith and Order Paper 214 (Geneva: WCC Publications, 2013), para. 52. See also *Episkopé and Episcopate in Ecumenical Perspective*, Faith and Order Paper 102 (Geneva: WCC Publications, 1980).

[34] *Meissen Agreement*, 15 ix. Cf. https://www.ekd.de/ekd_en/ds_doc/meissen_engl_.pdf (accessed 1 July 2021).

[35] Council for Christian Unity of the General Synod of the Church of England, *Together in Mission and Ministry : The Porvoo Common Statement, with Essays on Church and Ministry in Northern Europe* (London: Church House Publishing, 1993), 32 k.

[36] Anglican-Lutheran International Continuation Committee, *The Niagara Report. Report of the Anglican-Lutheran Consultation on Episcope*, Niagara Falls, September 1987 (London: Church House Publishing, 1988), 69.

[37] British and Irish Anglican Churches and the French Lutheran and Reformed Churches, 'Called to Witness and Service. The Reuilly Common Statement' (1999), in Sven Oppegaard, and Gregory Cameron (eds.), *Anglican-Lutheran Agreements*.

These examples demonstrate that this three-fold concept of oversight which originally derives from *BEM* (M 26) represents an agreement that subsequent ecumenical dialogues have acknowledged. These examples also show that the understanding of the EKD's identity and its significance for the understanding of episcopé have an impact on the EKD's relations with other churches. This is even clearer in the EKD's dialogue with the Roman Catholic Church and Orthodox Churches. In the dialogue between the EKD and the Russian Orthodox Church on 'The Episcopal Ministry in the Church' (*Der bischöfliche Dienst in der Kirche*) (1984), for example, the EKD's identity and its understanding of episcopé constitute reasons for crucial differences to the position of the Russian Orthodox Church. This is expressed especially in the joint theses on *Die Wahrnehmung der episkopé in der Kirche* which state how episcopé is understood and practised in the two churches.[38] These differences exist not only with regard to the understanding of episcopé, but also in relation to the relevance given to the understanding of episcopé for the unity of the church.[39]

Compared to these dialogues, the picture looks very different with regard to the EKD's dialogue with churches of the Reformation. For example, for the CPCE, which is based on a common understanding of the gospel, agreement on episcopé is not a condition for full communion in the sense of pulpit and table fellowship.[40] According to *The Church of Jesus Christ*,

---

Regional and International Agreements 1972–2002, LWF Documentation 49 (Geneva: LWF, 2004), 201–30, 46a vi.

[38] 'In the Orthodox Church, the episcopé is understood exclusively as the service of a bishop. In the Evangelical Church it is carried out partly by the bishop and partly through the cooperation of the bishop with synodical bodies' (Heinz Joachim Held and Klaus Schwarz (eds.), *Der bischöfliche Dienst in der Kirche. Eine Dokumentation über die zehnte Begegnung im bilateralen theologischen Dialog zwischen der Russischen Orthodoxen Kirche und der Evangelischen Kirche in Deutschland vom 25.–29. September 1984 in Kiev*, Beiheft zur Ökumenischen Rundschau 53 (Frankfurt: Verlag Otto Lembeck, 1992), 92–93.).

[39] As example for Lutheran-Roman Catholic dialogue, see, for example, Gerard Kelly, 'Episkope: A Recent Study of the Lutheran-Roman Catholic Dialogue in Australia', *One in Christ* 44/2 (2010), 153–67.

[40] See *Agreement between Reformation Churches in Europe (Leuenberg Agreement) 1973* (Frankfurt am Main: Verlag Otto Lembeck, 1993). See also William G. Rusch and Daniel F. Martensen (eds.), *The Leuenberg Agreement and Lutheran-Reformed Relationships: Evaluations by North American and European Theologians* (Minneapolis: Augsburg, 1989). Reviewed by H. G. Anderson, 'The Leuenberg Agreement and Lutheran–Reformed Relationships', *Lutheran Quarterly* 6/2 (1992): 226–7.

existing differences in the understanding of ministry and in the diverse shapes of ministry and service of episcopé 'do not call church fellowship in word and sacrament into question, since these differences do not refer to the foundation but to the shape of the church'[41]. Along the lines of the *Tampere Theses* (1987), differences in the structure of the church and its government are not necessarily an obstacle to church fellowship or to the reciprocal recognition of ministry and ordination, as long as the question of church governance remains subordinate to the sovereignty of the gospel.[42] Accordingly, the CPCE Study 'Ministry, ordination, episkopé and theological education' stresses that the term episcopé refers to the practice of pastoral oversight, with the purpose of ensuring both the 'being' (*esse*) of the church and its 'well being' (*bene esse*).[43] As the existence of episcopé is crucial, but not its very form, agreement on episcopé is not regarded as a church-dividing issue and as such not a condition for church unity.[44]

The dialogue between the EKD and the Church of England can be located between these two poles. As has been shown above, there is an episcopal dimension to church governance in the EKD. The functions of this episcopal dimension include both the task of preserving the apostolic faith through the ages, though it is not the only sign, as well as the *potestas ordinis*, the power of ordination. Here, this episcopal dimension is ecumenically relevant as these two functions are also functions of the episcopate in the Church of England. In short, for the Meissen dialogue, the EKD's identity and its impact on the significance of episcopé are of crucial importance.[45]

Another aspect of the EKD's perception of its identity with significance for episcopé which has potential for ecumenical cooperation is the importance of *diakonia*. This aspect has been very clearly expressed in the LWF's 'Lund Declaration' on the understanding of episcopé (2007). Though not an EKD document, it emphasizes the long-standing obligation of the

---

[41]   See Michael Bünker and Martin Friedrich (eds.), *The Church of Jesus Christ. The Contribution of the Reformation towards Ecumenical Dialogue on Church Unity*, Leuenberg Documents 1 (Leipzig: Evangelische Verlagsanstalt, fourth edition, 2012), 119.

[42]   See Tampere Theses 3, in: ibid., 117–119.

[43]   See *Ministry, ordination, episkopé and theological education*, 144.

[44]   See ibid., 35.

[45]   It will be very interesting to see whether and to what extent the dialogue between the Evangelical Lutheran Church in Bavaria and the Episcopal Church will affect the Meissen dialogue.

church, and especially its leadership, to care for the weak and needy. It clearly shows where episcopal leadership activities should be focused if the leadership does not want to lose itself in the preoccupation with itself and its own church institutions and bodies.[46]

3. Conclusion

When exploring how the perception of the EKD's identity affects its understanding of the significance of episcopé, including in its relations with other churches, it is essential to bear in mind that the EKD has developed from a *Kirchenbund* to a communion of twenty regional churches with Lutheran, Reformed and United confessional status. The development of the EKD's identity has also been influenced by ecumenical growth, most clearly in the context of the Leuenberg Church Fellowship. The development of the ecclesial identity of the EKD also shows the impact of the context in which its ecclesial identity has been formed, in other words, how non-doctrinal factors have influenced the shaping of the EKD's identity. The perception of the EKD's identity has a strong bearing on how the significance of episcopé is understood, as the examples from the EKD's ecumenical dialogues have illustrated.

---

[46]   See https://www.lutheranworld.org/resources?field_department_tid[]=6341&
field_department_tid[]=15&field_department_tid[]=14&field_department_tid%252
55B%25255D=14 (accessed 1 July 2021).

Why Synods? Why Bishops?

The Co-emergence of Synodical and Episcopal Forms of Church Governance (Episcopé) in German Lutheran Churches from 1918: Historical Factors, Theological Arguments. Constitutional Consequences

Bernd Oberdorfer

It might seem surprising that in German Lutheran Churches Synod and Bishop as two institutionalised forms of Church governance emerged (and actually co-emerged) only in the twentieth century. In particular, the end of monarchy after World War I resulted in a deep historical rupture for the Protestant churches. In this chapter, I will scrutinize the historical development, its theological rationale as well as its political and social background, referring in particular to the Evangelical-Lutheran Church in Bavaria. This is not for reasons of an indigenous Bavarian's localist pride. And of course, it does not imply that the Bavarian church is a case of outstanding best practice (which I would never dare say in the presence of Bishop Meister). Rather, I focus on Bavaria as being typical for the developments in the German Lutheran Churches. The crucial questions I would like to tackle are these: why exactly did the Bavarian Lutheran Church establish Synods? Why exactly were Bishops introduced as organs of Church governance in this phase of institutional reset? Was this based on theological arguments, or was it inspired by the transformation of the political system from monarchy to republic and democracy? And how did and does this Church describe the functions of these organs and their cooperation?

In the EKD-style setting of the Meissen Conference, a Lutheran approach indicates one side of the discussion. The developments in Lutheran churches are not necessarily typical of the United or Reformed churches. For example, on the one hand, in the Reformed tradition, synods were a common tool of church governance from the very beginning. And on the other hand, it was no accident that bishops were not included in Calvin's model of church ministries. This means that whereas the introduction of synods in Lutheran churches marks a convergence to Reformed ecclesiology, the introduction of bishops might appear as a distinctive Lutheran practice. But, as we will see, this is only partly true. Let us start with 'prehistory'.[1]

1. A Long Walk to Freedom? The Prehistory of an autonomous Luther- an Church in Bavaria

'In the beginning was Napoleon.' With these words, the historian Thomas Nipperday started his famous 3-volume *Deutsche Geschichte* of the nineteenth century.[2] This is also – indeed especially – true for Bavaria. After the end of the 'Holy Roman Empire of the German Nation' in 1803, Napoleon's politics of pressure and challenge brought about a widely new shape to the regional structure of the German territories. The 'Kingdom of Bavaria' which comprised more or less the same geographic regions as the 'Free State of Bavaria' today (excluding Coburg, but including the Palatinate) results from this fundamental change. Beforehand the Duchy of Bavaria with Munich as its capital comprised only the southeastern parts, to which were added Franconia in the North and Swabia in the West. The new political structure, however, also put an end to the principle of religious homogeneity of political territories which had been maintained since the Augsburg Religious Peace of 1555: *cuius regio eius religio*. The strictly catholic 'Old Bavaria' was unified now with strictly Lutheran regions (parts of Franconia, esp. Ansbach and Bayreuth),[3] Swabia was composed of small (some Catholic, some Lutheran, and a few Reformed) territories, and the Palatinate was Reformed (and later United). Thus, with respect to denominational structure, the Catholic King ruled a quite diverse Kingdom.

Strangely enough, however, one particular element of the old arrangement remained valid: the so-called *Landesherrliche Kirchenregiment*, i.e., the principle that in Protestant territories the political sovereign was at the same time the head of the regional church. In the new Bavaria, then, the Catholic King was *summus episcopus* of the Lutheran church. More-

---

[1] On this see, Werner K. Blessing, 'Minderheit im paritätischen Königreich. Eine Skizze zur rechtlichen, politischen und gesellschaftlichen Stellung der bayerischen Protestanten', in Hubertus Seibert (ed.), *Bayern und die Protestanten* (Regensburg: Friedrich Pustet, 2017), 154–175.

[2] Thomas Nipperdey, *Deutsche Geschichte 1800–1866* (München: C.H.Beck, 1983), 11.

[3] Other parts of Franconia, like Bamberg or Würzburg, were strictly Catholic.

over, the principle of the *Landesherrliche Kirchenregiment* required that the one King was in charge of only one (Lutheran) church. Thus, within the territory of the Kingdom of Bavaria, the different regional Lutheran churches established a common organisational structure: the 'Evangelical-Lutheran Church in Bavaria' – as it was later called – also results from the formation of the new political entity 'Kingdom of Bavaria'. This church was founded in 1808.

The king exercised his function as head of the Lutheran Church through an *Oberkonsistorium* (General Consistory) which was part of the administration, forming a part of the ministry of the interior. This *Oberkonsistorium*, located in Munich, was chaired by an *Oberkonsistorialpräsident* who could just as well be a legal expert as an ordained minister. It is interesting to note that the first *Oberkonsistorialräte* (councillors) were legal experts whereas later, ordained ministers were preferred (the first ordained theologian was Gottlieb Christoph Adolf von Harleß, in 1852).

Although it is clear that the Lutheran Church was not a State Church in the strict sense in that it was a minority church, it was nevertheless a church whose administration was part of the state administration. Theologically, this did not present any problems from the perspective of the Enlightenment paradigm which was dominant in the first decades of the 'new' church. But when, inspired by the romanticist idea of religion as a living tradition, a new consciousness of the confessional roots of Lutheran church and devotion arose, the integration of the church in the state bureaucracy could be judged as compromising the specifically *religious* character of the church. Wilhelm Löhe, for example, the founder of the diaconical institutions in Neuendettelsau and an influential proponent of a confessionalist revival, considered the option of separating from the state-subsided church and establishing a strictly Lutheran 'free church', but decided to stay and reform the church 'from the inside'.

All this meant that there was a growing awareness of the lack of ecclesial self-governance. It is no accident that in 1849 after the ultimately unsuccessful liberal revolution this led to the establishment of (regional and general) synods. These were composed of 50 per cent pastors and 50 per cent lay members. This balance was later adjusted to one third pastors and two thirds lay members, all of them, of course, male,[4] and meeting every three years. The synod was deliberately conceived not as decision-

---

4   Women could be elected to the Synod only from 1958.

making body but rather as an advisory board representing the regional diversity and ensuring member participation.

This was the situation of the Lutheran Church's governance before monarchy came to an end:

- the Catholic king as *summus episcopus* who did not unfold doctrinal or liturgical authority;
- the *Oberkonsistorium* as administrative office, chaired by a *Oberkonsistorialpräsident* who did not function as bishop but increasingly was recognised as the public representative of the Church;
- and the *Synod* as an advisory board without formal legislative or executive rights, even though, according to an unbinding rule, any important topic was supposed to be submitted to the Synod for its attention and discussion.

This configuration mirrors the fact that Lutheran churches traditionally did not pay too much attention to supra-regional and supra-parochial structures of Church governance and maintained a more or less pragmatic attitude towards them. This does not mean that there was no awareness of the need for spiritual and doctrinal oversight. There was no question that ordained ministry was central to the essence of the Church and had an indispensable responsibility to safeguard the Church's loyalty to its apostolic sources. And as to doctrinal questions, the contribution of the Theological Faculties to the *magisterium* of the church was highlighted. But there was no need of developing more comprehensive normative theological models of church government (*episcopé*) until the collapse of the *Landesherrliche Kirchenregiment*.

2. Reset: The Restructuring of the Landeskirche after 1918

The end of Monarchy in the German Empire and all of its territories in 1918 – in Bavaria the King abdicated on 13 November – essentially changed the setting of the churches within the state.[5] In Bavaria, on 14 January 1919, the provisional 'State Constitution of the Republic of Bavaria'

5   On what follows, see Hans-Peter Hübner, 'Neuordnung der Evangelisch-Lutherischen Landeskirche und ihres Verhältnisses zum Staat', in Gerhard Müller et al (eds), *Handbuch der Geschichte der Evangelischen Kirche in Bayern. Bd.2: 1800–2000* (St. Ottilien: EOS-Verl., 2000), 211–232.

(*Staatsgrundgesetz der Republik Bayern*) guaranteed the 'religious associations' (*Glaubensgesellschaften*) 'independence from the State' (art. 14). On 17 March 1919, the 'Provisional Constitution of the Free State of Bavaria' (*Vorläufiges Staatsgrundgesetz des Freistaats Bayern*) confirmed this, adding that the religious associations 'arrange and administer their affairs autonomously in accordance with the state laws' (art. 15). At a national level, on 11 August 1919, The *Weimarer Reichsverfassung* (Weimar Constitution) declared 'There is no State church' and underlined the autonomy of the Church's self- governance. However, instead of equating religious associations to private clubs, churches were given a specific public status. This meant that the separation of Church and State in Germany, unlike in France, did not result in a strict secularism. These principles were incorporated in the so-called Bavarian "Bamberg Constitution" of 14 August 1919.

On the basis of this, the Bavarian Parliament, on 2 February 1920, officially declared the *Landesherrliche Kirchenregiment* to be abolished, after, on 28 January 1920, the Bavarian Government had suspended the General Consistory as a State office.

This challenged the *Landeskirche* to build up structures of self-governance. The church had to reinvent itself, as it were. That did not mean, however, that it had to start from scratch. But the institutional structures had to be adapted to the new setting and were substantially transformed. After long discussions, the *Kirchenverfassung* [Church Constitution] of September 1920, which came into force in 1921 demonstrated the new structure:

- Firstly, the status of the Synod was massively raised. The *Landessynode* (which replaced the *Generalsynode*) was no longer only an advisory board but now had legislative competence which had hitherto been in the hands of the State. The Synod was presided over by a lay member.
- Secondly, a *Landessynodalausschuss* [Standing Commission of the Synod] was established in order to transact synodical business between the Meetings of the Synod.
- Thirdly, a *Landeskirchenrat* [Church Council] replaced the *Oberkonsistorium* as the administrative board of the Church.

The first draft of the Church Constitution mentioned only these three organs of self-governance. But soon a majority felt that there was a lack of a personal representative for the Church in this model which resulted in a desire to have a representative who would more or less combine the functions of *Summus Episcopus* and *Oberkonsistorialpräsident*. This meant that a fourth instrument of church governance was introduced. There was discussion as to whether this would be called *Landesbischof*, but it was finally decided to use the term *Kirchenpräsident* which more clearly demonstrated the continuity with the office of the *Oberkonsistorialpräsident*. Nevertheless, the intention was to have a more 'bishop-like' person representing the church.

In the Church Constitution of 1920, these four instruments are located on the same level without degrees of hierarchy. As to the Synod, writings on Canon Law tended to avoid parallels to political parliaments. It was argued that a Synod had no 'parties' which try to enforce their particular interests against those of other 'parties' but instead all members share in the responsibility for the common good. But this reveals a somewhat negative picture of decision-making in democratic parliaments and at the same time an unrealistic and overly harmonious picture of decision-making in the Church. Moreover, it is evident that the Synod is designed to represent the diversity within the Church and to foster member participation in Church governance, both of which it has in common with political parliaments.

From a more negative point of view, this connection with the political process becomes even more evident when we take into consideration that in 1933, in the context of the National Socialist *Machtergreifung* [seizure of power], the competences of the Synod were restricted by an *Ermächtigungsgesetz* [Enabling Act] which enormously strengthened the position of the *Kirchenpräsident* who was given the title of *Landesbischof*. It was no accident that the Synod did not meet from 1934 to 1946. The motives behind this change were ambiguous: On the one hand, the anti-democratic, authoritarian *zeitgeist* was also popular in the Church with many Protestants supporting the Nazi programme. This meant that there was a desire for a strong leader figure in the Church and an antipathy towards the culture of constructive parliamentary debate. On the other hand, choosing the title *Landesbischof* indicated the intention to distinguish *spiritual* authority from *political* authority. Consequently, at least in part, it did not aim at adapting the Church to the political order but rather at emphasising the specifically religious character of the Church. This would serve to safeguard the Church against the enforcement of Nazi totalitarianism [*Gleichschaltung*]. Similarly, one of the reasons not to convene the Synod for many years was to prevent the Church from the influence of Synod members who were openly sympathetic to Nazi ideology.

It is interesting to note that in 1946, after the end of the Nazi era, Hans Meiser, who was elected as *Landesbischof* in 1933 after the resignation of *Kirchenpräsident* Friedrich Veit, abolished the Enabling Act returning constitutional rights to the Synod. The title *Landesbischof*, however, remained (and, needless to say, Meiser remained in office).

Let us jump now from history into the present day. What are the functions of *Landesbischof* and *Landessynode*, according to the Church Constitution in its revised version of 1971 which remains in force until today (including some minor modifications)? And how is the cooperation of these different organs regulated?

3. Checks and Balances? The Polycentric Structure of Church-Governance

The 1971 revision of the Church Constitution did not implement substantial structural changes but adapted the description of the organs of Church Government to what might be described as more 'Habermasian' *zeitgeist*.[6] Firstly, whereas the Constitution of 1920 had only declared *Kirchenpräsident/Landesbischof* and *Landeskirchenrat* explicitly to be 'Church-leading organs', the Constitution now included *Landessynode* and *Landessynodalausschuss* into this category. This highlights the fact that Church Government is not exclusively exercised by the ordained ministry, something to which I shall return. Secondly, the 1971 Constitution did not place the instruments of government in any sort of hierarchy. They perform the governance of the Church *together*, 'in a community with a division of labour and mutual responsibility' [*arbeitsteilige Gemeinschaft und wechselseitige Verantwortung*]. Together, they are 'responsible for seeing that the Evangelical-Lutheran Church in Bavaria fulfils its duties in doctrine and life, proclamation and pastoral care, organisation and administration and preserves its unity and freedom' (art. 41 '[2]').[7] The economic term 'division

---

[6]   On this, see my more extensive discussion in Bernd Oberdorfer, 'Arbeitsteilige Gemeinschaft und gegenseitige Verantwortung. Zum Verhältnis von synodaler und bischöflicher Episkope im gegenwärtigen Luthertum', in Gunther Wenz et al. (eds.), *Ekklesiologie und Kirchenverfassung. Die institutionelle Gestalt des episkopalen Dienstes* (Münster etc.: LIT, 2003), 123–136.

[7]   *All* the institutions of Church governance are *jointly* 'verantwortlich, dass die Evangelisch-Lutherische Kirche in Bayern in Lehre und Leben, Verkündigung und Seelsorge, Ordnung und Verwaltung ihre Aufgabe erfüllt und ihre Einheit und Freiheit wahrt' (Art. 41 [2]). The Consitution is at: https://www.bayern-evangelisch.de/downloads/ELKB_Kirchenverfassung_Stand_2020.pdf (accessed 21 March 2022).

of labour' indicates that they exercise different functions and their duties are not interchangeable. Nevertheless, the task of preserving the unity of the Church, for example, is not exclusively ascribed to the bishop. And, moreover, the synod is not given merely a second-level responsibility: 'The *Landessynode*,' the Constitution reads (art. 43 [1]), 'can negotiate all church issues and, by doing so, take decisions on tasks which result from the mission of the Church in the [reality of the] Evangelical Lutheran Church of Bavaria'.[8] And, because 'Church governance is a spiritual and at the same time legal service',[9] the responsibility of the synod cannot be restricted to organisational issues and the bishop's competence limited to spiritual and doctrinal issues.

We now outline how the respective specific functions of *Landesbischof* and *Landessynode* are described in the Constitution. The Constitution lists ten 'duties of the *Landesbischof*'.[10] The first one is: 'He [or she] sees that the Word of God is proclaimed in accordance with Holy Scripture and the [Lutheran] Confessions and that the sacraments are rightly administered.'[11] After this fundamental function – which refers to the Augsburg Confession, art. 7, and highlights the core mission of the Church as a whole as well as the specific vocation of the ordained ministry – the Constitution names administrative tasks (e. g., the enforcement of church laws and the appointment of pastors and Church officers) and adds an extensive list of pastoral functions such as counselling or inspiring dialogue and different ways of conversation. The clear intention is not to give the picture of a hierarchical, authoritarian Church leader but rather an integrative mediator, spiritual counsellor and public 'face' of the church. As to doctrinal authority, the Constitution gives the *Landesbischof* the right of veto against decisions of the *Landessynode* by suspending the synod and ordering a new election. But if the new synod repeats the earlier decision, the Bishop cannot repeat his or her veto. This means that the veto is only provisional and not decisive in itself. It is interesting to note that the Con-

---

8   'Die Landessynode kann über alle kirchlichen Angelegenheiten verhandeln und dabei über Aufgaben beschließen, die sich aus dem Auftrag der Kirche für die Evangelisch-Lutherische Kirche in Bayern ergeben.' (Art. 43 [1])
9   'In der Evangelisch-Lutherischen Kirche in Bayern ist Leitung der Kirche zugleich geistlicher und rechtlicher Dienst.' (Art. 5)
10 See art. 61 (1). The current version reads 'Landesbischof bzw. [...] Landesbischöfin'. The gender-inclusive language was added after the introduction of the ordination of women in 1976.
11 Art. 61 (1) 1: 'Er bzw. sie achtet darauf, dass das Wort Gottes schrift- und bekenntnisgemäß verkündigt wird und die Sakramente recht verwaltet werden.'

stitution does not include ordination in this list of duties but speaks of the 'right of ordination and visitation' in a separate sub-paragraph (art. 61 [2]). This might indicate that ordination is not regarded as an aspect of Church-governance but forms a category of its own.[12]

The *Landessynode*, according to the Constitution, is 'assigned to joint decision-making of the Evangelical Lutheran Church in Bavaria" (art. 42 [1]).[13] It 'embodies the unity and diversity of the congregations, institutions, and services' of the Church. It thus mirrors and represents the communion. The list of its duties starts with 'the right of Church legislation' and the election of the *Landesbischof* (art. 43[2]) and continues with different issues of decision-making, in such matters as the introduction of liturgies or hymn books, or the creation of new parishes, or on the budget of the church.

To come to an end: Of course, as already said, the functions of *Landesbischof* and *Landessynode* are not identical. It is no accident that the Bishop is neither a member nor head of the Synod. But in relation to the governance of the Church, there is no priority given to the Bishop. The idea is that the institutions of Church leadership perform *episcopé* together, avoiding controversies, and forming consensus. This mirrors the distinction that Canon Law Theory draws between the basic function of the ordained ministry – publicly proclaiming the Gospel and administering the sacraments – and the function of *episcopé* which is not an exclusive competence of the ordained ministry.

---

[12]   The Constitution does not develop a theory of ordination. It only names the *Landesbischof* and the *Oberkirchenräte im Kirchenkreis* (regional senior administrators who can be addressed as *Regionalbischöfe*, but only within their respective region) as persons who have the right or duty to ordain. But it does not emphasise that these persons have this right or duty exclusively. In the article on 'the calling to publicly proclaiming the Word of God and administering the sacraments' it only reads that persons are called into this office 'by laying on of hands, blessing and sending' (art. 13) in 'good order' without explicit reference to the persons who are entitled to perform this 'orderly call'.

[13]   The synod is 'zur gemeinsamen Willensbildung der Evangelisch-Lutherischen Kirche in Bayern berufen' (Art. 42 [1]).

Moving forward

A vision for Meissen on the 'interchangeability of ministers'
and 'reconciliation of ministries'

Matthias Grebe with Jonathan Gibbs

Introduction

2021 saw the celebration of the thirtieth anniversary of the Meissen Declaration – though of course the conversations started earlier. From 1985
onwards, official delegates were appointed by the Church of England, the
Federation of the Evangelical Churches in the German Democratic Republic and the Evangelical Church in Germany (EKD) in the Federal Republic
of Germany to work out a basis for closer relations. It was in 1988 in
Meissen that conversations between delegations from these three bodies
produced an Agreement between the churches. And in November 1988
the General Synod of the Church of England welcomed the Meissen Common Statement calling for a closer relationship between the Church of
England and the EKD and an Act of Synod proclaimed the Meissen Declaration in January 1991.

In light of the history of Meissen and its thirtieth anniversary celebration, this paper takes a fresh look at the rationale of the Meissen work,
asking what it wants to 'achieve', why it matters, and how it is to be practically worked out in the coming years. It is no secret that the consensus
established in the Meissen Declaration is sufficient for the EKD to 'enter
into full church fellowship unreservedly and without qualifications,'[1] since
the fundamental church-constituting features are all guaranteed in Meis-

---

[1] Ingolf Dalferth, 'Ministry and the Office of Bishop according to Meissen and Porvoo:
Protestant Remarks about Several Unclarified Questions', in *Visible Unity and the
Ministry of Oversight:* The Second Theological Conference held under the Meissen
Agreement between the Church of England and the Evangelical Church in Ger-
many, West Wickham, March 1996 (London: Church House Publishing, 1997),
9–48, 10.

sen. The reservation is on the Church of England, rather than the EKD side.[2] In order to deepen the conversation, and building on the work of previous years, the Commission from the Church of England side organised a Meissen-led Colloquium for ecumenical guests in 2021, with the overall aim of bringing together ecumenical colleagues and Meissen partners in a discussion around the theme of 'Identity' in the context of the ongoing exploration of the mutual recognition of ministries between our Churches.

In a first step, this paper will give an answer to the pressing questions raised. In a second, it will outline the discussion that took place at the Meissen-led Colloquium; and finally, it will look to evaluate the conversations that took place in light of next possible steps which can realistically be achieved.

The rationale: interchangeability of ministries and Christian unity

By signing the Declaration (VI. Mutual acknowledgement and next steps), the EKD and the Church of England recognised each other as Churches belonging to the One, Holy, Catholic and Apostolic Church of Jesus Christ, committing to journeying towards closer fellowship in as many areas of Christian life and witness as possible. The provision allows for a much closer degree of fellowship (pulpit and altar fellowship, though not the interchangeability of ministries) and commits the signatory Churches to work for the goal of full, visible unity of the Church.

A body for Church of England-EKD relations known as the Meissen Commission works together by taking part in annual exchanges of delegations and representatives. Another key part of the Meissen work has been to carry forward the theological dialogue, with a view to resolving the outstanding differences between our two traditions. To this end, the Meissen process also includes the Meissen Theological Conferences. These 'forms of joint oversight' now bind the Church of England and the EKD together, and ensure that the Meissen Agreement will have practical consequences for the life of the Churches.

---

[2]   There is 'presently no legal obstacle to a priest of the Church of England being invited as a visitor to preach or celebrate the sacraments in any of the member churches of the EDK', in Axel Freiherr von Campenhausen and Augur Pearce, 'Legal Annex: Interchangeability of Ministries between the Church of England and the member churches of the EKD – The Present Legal Position', in *Visible Unity and the Ministry of Oversight*, 5–6, 5.

Within European ecumenical dialogue, the Agreement between the two Churches remains a model for other ecumenical agreements and is set out in the *Meissen Common Statement: On the Way to Visible Unity*. The Agreement contains a joint declaration known as the Meissen Declaration. The importance of the Meissen work transcends church structures and always has to be considered in the wider context of the new Europe in the twentieth century. The Declaration was a result of ecumenical dialogue between those who lived through World War II and was designed in direct response to the events of Coventry and Dresden by those who witnessed and learned from these tragedies.

Ten areas of agreement on the fundamentals of the faith are covered: Scripture, the Creeds, justification and sanctification, the nature of the Church, worship and sacramental life, baptism and the Eucharist, the corporate priesthood of the whole people of God, ordered ministry and oversight exercised in personal, collegial and communal ways, and hope in the final consummation of the Kingdom.

Chapter V of the *Meissen Common Statement* sets out in 10 points some agreements in faith, but notes in paragraph 16 one remaining difference – over the historic Episcopal succession, which prevents the mutual recognition of ministries in the Meissen Declaration from resulting in a full inter-changeability of ministries. Thus, the Meissen work is focused on the full interchangeability of ministers (as opposed to only recognition),[3] i.e. the full reconciliation between the ordained ministries of the Church of England and the EKD.

Historically, for the Anglican Church to safeguard and spread the Gospel effectively in England it 'required the retention of the historic three-fold orders.'[4] For Anglicans, ordained ministry is essential to the Church and the 'recognition that the ordained ministry is a distinctive gift of the Spirit is part of what makes a church a true part of the catholic Church.'[5] Furthermore, although 'Anglican ecumenical documents have

---

[3]   See Ingolf Dalferth, 'Ministry and the Office of Bishop according to Meissen and Porvoo: Protestant Remarks about several unclarified questions', in *Visible Unity and the Ministry of Oversight*, 17 f.

[4]   Matthias Grebe, 'What Constitutes a Church? Revisiting Ecclesiology, Ordained Ministry, and Episcopé in light of the Meissen Declaration', in Mark Chapman, Friederike Nüssel, and Matthias Grebe (eds), *Revisiting the Meissen Declaration after 30 Years* (Leipzig: Evangelische Verlagsanstalt, 2020), 33.

[5]   *Recognition by the Church of England or orders conferred in other churches* (Faith and Order Commission), 6.

always emphasised that this historic Episcopate is not essential to its being a true church, Anglican ecclesiology maintains that the ministry of bishops provides a link between the local church and the universal Church, as witnessed throughout history when bishops met to take counsel together.'[6]

Anglican bishops meet together 'collegially at provincial level and, through the Lambeth Conference, at world level.'[7] Thus, bishops are seen as organs of church unity and the link of continuity with historical events. Furthermore, in the Church of England, 'episcopal ordination is a canonical requirement for serving as an ordained minister'[8] since the Act of Uniformity of 1662 and significant legal changes would be needed for a non-episcopally ordained minister to be eligible to exercise ordained ministry in the Church of England.[9] So whether or not one agrees with the practice of admitting a non-episcopally ordained minister into a benefice, as was occasionally done before 1662,[10] it became no longer legally possible after the Act of Uniformity of 1662.

The *Chicago Quadrilateral* of 1886 sets out four fundamental pre-requisites for church union, points which were adopted in 1888 at the Lambeth Conference: (1) the Scriptures of Old and New Testament, (2) the Apostles' Creed and Nicene Creed, (3) the Sacraments of baptism and eucharist, and finally (4) 'The Historic Episcopate, locally adapted in the methods of its administration to the varying needs of the nations and peoples called of God into the Unity of His Church.'[11] The fourth point on the historic Episcopate in the *Chicago-Lambeth Quadrilateral* appears to be

---

6 Grebe, 'What Constitutes a Church?', 33.

7 *Mission and Ministry in Covenant*: Report from The Faith and Order bodies of the Church of England and the Methodist Church, §39b.

8 *MMC*, §54.

9 The Anglican-Methodist Covenant proposes a solution to this problem which require no amendment of the 1662 Act or other related Canons: 'it is proposed that the Church of England, in response to the Methodist Church receiving the historic episcopate, introduce legislation that would in effect dispense Methodist presbyters for a limited period from the requirement to have received episcopal ordination in order to serve by invitation in the Church of England,' in *MMC*, §75.

10 See Stephen Hampton, 'The Synod of Dordrecht and the re-protestantization of the Church of England', in by Mark Chapman, Friederike Nüssel, and Matthias Grebe (eds), *Revisiting the Meissen Declaration after 30 Years* (Leipzig: Evangelische Verlagsanstalt, 2020), 75f., who gives various historical examples where this took place.

11 *The Chicago-Lambeth Quadrilateral.* Resolution 11, (d) of the 1888 Lambeth Confernce.

the real stumbling block, curtailing the reconciliation of ministries between the Church of England and the EKD. And Ingolf Dalferth is right in his evaluation of the current situation of Meissen, that full, visible unity all depends on the one question of the historic episcopate,[12] as for the Church of England the interchangeability of ministers is 'not possible without an agreement on the interchangeability of episcopal ministers.'[13]

Having said this, however, it also needs highlighting that 'the Church of England as a whole has never committed itself to the view that the episcopate is of the *esse* of the Church.'[14] Nevertheless, if both Churches agree that they participate in the 'One, Holy, Catholic and Apostolic Church of Jesus Christ (para. 17 A (i)), and if ordained ministry is constitutive and essential for the Church (para. 15 (viii)), then this participation extends to the ordained ministry of the church concerned.'[15] So Dalferth asks a key question: 'where does the *theological* difference between Protestant and Anglican ordination lie, which hinders us from speaking not only of mutual recognition, but also of full reconciliation of ministries? What theological quality does the Anglican *conferring of Holy Orders* possess, which is missing from the Protestant calling to the ordained ministry?'[16] To address this question squarely, the Meissen work over the last five years has raised questions about a right understanding of the relationship between episcopé and the Church, culminating in the invitation to ecumenical partners to participate in the 2021 Colloquium, to which we now turn.

---

[12] See Ingolf Dalferth, 'Visible Unity and the Episcopal Office', in Ingolf U. Dalferth and Paul Oppenheim, Einheit bezeugen / Witnessing to Unity (Frankfurt: Lembeck, 2003), 207–218, 208–9.

[13] *Receiving One Another's Ordained Ministries: The Inter-Anglican Standing Commission on Unity, Faith and Order* (April 2016), 3. At: https://www.anglicancommunion.org/media/311030/ACC-16-Receiving-One-Anothers-Ordained-Ministries.pdf (accessed 21 March 2022).

[14] *Episcopal Ministry: The Report of the Archbishops' Group on the Episcopate* (London: Church House Publishing, 1990), § 188.

[15] Ingolf Dalferth, 'Ministry and the Office of Bishop according to Meissen and Porvoo: Protestant Remarks about Several Unclarified Questions', in *Visible Unity and the Ministry of Oversight:* The Second Theological Conference held under the Meissen Agreement between the Church of England and the Evangelical Church in Germany, West Wickham, March 1996 (London: Church House Publishing, 1997), 40.

[16] Dalferth, 'Ministry and the Office', 17.

The 'Meissen-led Colloquium' on 'Identity':
Listening to diverse ecumenical voices

The *Meissen-led Colloquium* was a virtual meeting with the overarching theme of 'Identity', which took place on 5-6 July 2021. The inclusion of different voices in the ongoing Meissen work towards interchangeability of ministers and full reconciliation of ministries promoted greater understanding of our differences and points of intersection, and facilitated further progress towards deeper unity (John 17). Members of the Church of England, Evangelische Kirche Deutschland, Roman Catholic Church, Methodist Church, United Reformed Church, Church of Finland, Church of Denmark, Church of Scotland, French Protestant Church and representatives from the Church of England's Council for Christian Unity, Conference of European Churches, Reuilly (the Church of England discussions with the French Protestant Churches), Porvoo (the Anglican Churches of the British Isles and the Nordic Lutheran Churches), and Communion of Protestant Churches in Europe were present. The keynote speaker was the New Testament scholar, John Barclay, Lightfoot Professor of Divinity at Durham University, who addressed the group on 'Church and Identity in the Writings of Paul'.

A brief overview of the two days of the Colloquium

Jonathan Gibbs, Bishop of Huddersfield in the Diocese of Leeds, Lead Safeguarding Bishop for the Church of England and Co-Chair of the Meissen Commission opened the Colloquium and welcomed everybody, outlining the reasons for focusing on the theme of Identity and expressing his hopes for this unique meeting in taking forward the objectives of the Meissen Declaration. Professor John Barclay gave the first address on the 'Church and Identity in the Writings of Paul', entitled *The Message and its Bearers* which surveyed two bodies of text, the undisputed letters of Paul (Romans; 1 and 2 Corinthians; Galatians; 1 Thessalonians; Philippians; Philemon) and the Pastoral Epistles (deutero-Pauline: 1 and 2 Timothy; Titus). He also addressed the historical and ecclesial contexts, and stressed that both are part of the New Testament canon. He emphasized the importance of Networks and Traditions using the illustration of Rhizomatic and Arboreal networks, to explain the spread, coalescence, and control of the early Christian movement.

Among other contributions was that of Richard Clutterbuck, who spoke on different aspects of Methodist identity, focusing on organisational identity (the principles of Connexionalism and Conference); doctrinal identity (Scripture, tradition, reason and experience based on the 'fundamental truths of the Protestant Reformation' and emphasising the priesthood of all believers); and cultural identity where it often pitched itself against the Church of England. He also looked at the Covenant arrangement between Anglicans and Methodists in Ireland, where it was relatively easy to arrange for the interchangeability of ordained ministries, even without Methodism adopting a formal episcopate in the historic succession. This presented fewer problems in the predominantly lower church tradition of the Church of Ireland. What now happens is that each year's Methodist President is installed and consecrated in a service which involves Anglican bishops as well as Methodist leaders, and where the liturgy refers to 'episcopal minister'.

In her talk, Johanna Rahner, a Roman Catholic Professor from the University of Tübingen, expounded the thesis that the Roman Catholic Church defines itself explicitly as a *communio hierarchica* (a hierarchically-structured church). It has a specific dialectic of episcopal and papal authority, and regards the episcopal office as the central criterion of being a 'Church in the proper sense', including when evaluating other denominations. In her exposition she made some important historical observations: first, it was only from the seventeenth century that the idea that a lack of apostolic succession became 'an indication for the invalidity of an ordination or the eucharist'. Second, from Trent there was a strong emphasis on the pastoral dimension of episcopacy which flourished at the Enlightenment. Third, however, from the nineteenth century there was an almost complete recasting of the episcopal office from a papalist perspective. Fourth, the speed of communication meant that papal dominance expanded further into catholic life than ever before, which had not fundamentally changed since Vatican II. What was clear was that there was a gap between the history of episcopacy and its doctrine, especially in relation to the role of synods in electing bishops and defining doctrine. This brought to light the central importance of the relation of the local to the universal.

From a different perspective the Lutheran Bishop Matti Repo of the Diocese of Tempere in Finland spoke on 'Identity and Episcope' in relation to the early Anglican-Lutheran discussions between the Churches of England and Finland. These began in the 1930s and resulted in what was then called an 'economic intercommunion' – or what would be referred to as eucharistic hospitality in today's ecumenical vocabulary. He noted, however, that the Anglican party, while acknowledging the bishops of the

Church of Finland as standing in historic continuity, the fact that in exceptional cases deans were legally allowed to preside over ordination of priests meant that no agreement on interchangeability of ministries could be reached in 1936. It was not until five years after adopting the Porvoo Declaration in 1996 that the General Synod abolished presbyteral ordinations.

After the Second War, Repo went on, the identity of the Evangelical Lutheran Church of Finland began to change from a pietistic, nationally-oriented, and low-church-type of thinking into an ecumenical, international, and more sacramental, liturgical, and, when it comes to the episcopé, a 'charismatic' understanding. The episcopal ministry was understood less in an administrative context and more as representing spiritual oversight in preaching and presiding over the Eucharist and consulting with the clergy. This development took place at the same time as the overall development into a more democratically-governed church.

Repo went on to discuss the importance of episcopé in Lutheran identity, pointing to the study by the Ecumenical Institute at Strasbourg, *Lutherische Identität / Lutheran Identity*, which emphasized the 'personal, collegial, and communal' aspects of episcope:

> [The] supra-regional ministers have taken different forms according to their time and place. In this way structures developed in which the responsibility for supra-regional direction and oversight was exercised in a personal manner (by bishops or church presidents), in a collegial manner (by cooperation among church leaders or the conference of bishops), and in a synodical manner (by synod gatherings including non-ordained persons). Episcope is not always exercised solely by an *episkopos* (that is, bishop) but through the interaction of different persons and institutions in charge of the direction of the church.[17]

What was important was that the 'personal way of exercising the episcope underlines the charismatic nature of the ministry', which was based on the invocation of the Holy Spirit in the epicletic prayer and imposition of hands during the ordination liturgy. This pneumatological element of episcopé is embedded in the personal and collegial forms of oversight, but it is not as evidently part of the communal form, which could easily become overly managerialised.

[17]   *Lutherische Identität / Lutheran Identity* (Leipzig: Evangelische Verlagshaus, 2019), 34.

From a wider Anglican perspective, Will Adam, Director of Unity, Faith and Order and Deputy Secretary General of the Anglican Communion, highlighted that the nature and character of the bishop, the historic episcopacy and the episcopal ordering of the Church have shaped the identity and self-understanding of Anglicans, both in relationships within their churches and the worldwide Communion, as well as between Anglicans and other Churches. He discussed a number of key aspects of history to explore the survival of episcopacy through the Reformation, where from 1558 a reformed episcopate worked with and in Parliament in the governance of the state in line with the Tudor worldview of a commonwealth of Godly Prince and faithful Church. In 1662 following the Civil Wars there was a reassertion of the threefold order of ministry and the insistence that those presbyters not episcopally ordained be so ordained in order to keep on in their ministry, which reaffirmed the historic episcopate as integral to ecclesial identity. From the nineteenth century the Tractarians identified Anglicanism more closely with the ancient Church, emphasising the one tangible thing to which they could point that demonstrated this connection: the historic episcopate. Internationally, the episcopal character and diocesan organisation of Anglicanism became a determinative constant, which is demonstrated in the Lambeth Conference as well as the other so-called 'instruments of communion'.

Nevertheless, he went on, despite its undeniable episcopal character, Anglicanism has always had a distinctive role for the laity. In the early days of English Anglicanism the monarch had a clear role, but Monarchs from Henry VIII onwards managed ecclesiastical affairs with and through parliament in which Bishops were a part, but only a small part, alongside laity. The synods of Anglican Churches around the world contain representation of bishops, clergy and laity and many have systems of checks and balances that prevent one house from imposing its will against the wishes of another.

Points for reflection

In the context of the discussions of the various inputs, especially those of John Barclay, there were a number of important points that emerged. First, Christian unity is rooted in the sacraments of Baptism and the Eucharist, which is a repeated motif in Paul's letters. The Words of Consecration are words echoing those of Jesus himself at his Last Supper: 'This is my body, given for you' is what gives the Church dignity and worth to all members of the community. We are who we are in our new *relationship* to Christ – one body – rather than individualised. Our new existence in Christ is given a completely new shape. This means that our continuing encounter with Christ in faith is continually reshaping our narrative of identity, which is reflected in the biblical narrative. The Church is a community in the process of *becoming*, being transformed by the Spirit, and therefore we need to recognise the historicization of ourselves and our Churches.

An important question here was this: when we look at the worldwide Church and its various traditions, what do we do about identities being formed in opposition to one another? Even though it is natural that we define ourselves against others, we need to be aware that we do not make it our primary mode of definition to be different from others and that we do not absolutize our differences. Instead, we need to be conscious of the fact that we all belong to one body and can learn from each other.

If one moves on to Paul and the image of the olive tree in Romans 9–11, there is a danger of thinking that one tradition is the basic, and therefore the best one, into which others are grafted. For Paul, the root is the grace and mercy of God. This mirrors Paul's attempt to point back from the church to its source in the Christ-event. The Church has to define itself by its source in God rather than by its institutional structure. However, there is a residual tension in the Christian tradition: we are always pointing beyond ourselves, but in doing so, we cannot avoid the specificity and particularity in language, thought, and structure. From the beginning of the early Church, thought-patterns were also shaped by the context in which they spread. This means that there is an interesting diversity in early Christianity.

In light of the many cultural differences even within the EKD itself, many questions were raised. Can the Porvoo model help the Meissen process out of its impasse? Does the Leuenberg model actually describe where we are in reality? Can we say that the episcopate in Lutheran ecclesiology is to safeguard continuity when for centuries the Lutheran Church did not have episcopacy? For the Lutheran Church it was historically not only episcopacy that safeguarded continuity; this safeguard was part of something much broader. What was emphasized was that the EKD needs to learn from plurality in their own churches when discussing ecumenical topics.

At the same time, in the Anglican context and the wider Communion there is also no unified experience of bishops. While there seems to be a tendency to see the Church of England as the 'Anglican way', this of course obscures the entire picture, as the experience of episcopacy around the Communion is very different. Episcopé is embedded and exercised in personal, collegial, and communal oversight. The latter form is one of the key questions that requires discussion within the Meissen work, as there appears to be a tension between the communal and the personal dimensions. How can communal episcopacy be exercised in an ecumenical dialogue? In particular, resolution needs to be sought in the pneumatological dimension. There is a fundamental challenge posed in the question of how to live according to the Spirit – which is not always obvious in our synodical structures –, and how to discern the will of God as expressed through the people of God. Discussion of these aspects of episcopé leads to further reflection on the question of authority and power, and where this resides in churches.

Further questions, reflections and possible next steps

The diverse group of people who gathered online for the Colloquium created what was a quite unique ecumenical event, as well as a very productive example of what dialogue across different traditions and disciplines can help to bring. It was truly an example of 'theology on the way' – of walking together and working together to ask different questions that might in due course lead to new answers to old problems. In this spirit of asking questions rather than giving answers, we would like to end this short paper with some of the issues that we believe could be explored further, as we seek to live out our Lord's prayer for the Church that we should be one, even as the Father and the Son are one (John 17). We hope the shared experience outlined here, together with these ongoing questions, may stimulate further exploration and promote deeper mutual understanding and co-operation between all of our Churches. Of course, these questions are themselves not exhaustive and should above all be read as an invitation to further engagement:

– Are all the differences between the Church of England and EKD theological or are there any non-theological factors here? A potential next step could be to explore the non-theological factors that affect our understanding of our denominations.

– Alongside the non-theological factors, we also need greater precision in our theological language to clearly define what we really mean by, for example, the distinction between episcopé and episcopacy?

– The different gifts of authority need further exploration, with a deeper evaluation of what is already done well in collegial, personal and communal authority. What other signs of continuity are there that bind churches together?

– Meissen also needs to reflect more deeply on the practical theology of episcopacy: what does it look like 'on the ground' and how does this relate to other factors of oversight? Here the question was raised about what Meissen can learn from the dialogue between the Bavarian Church and the Episcopal Church.

– Given that a number of EKD member churches already have *Landesbischöfe*, could the embrace of the historic Episcopate be seen by the EKD as a 'bearable anomaly', to adopt a term used by the Church of England-Methodist dialogue?

– In the same light it was said that we need to continue to challenge one another. What is required is ruthless honesty and a willingness to ask 'What are we holding onto, why, and is it essential?'

Ultimately, all participants agreed that it will only be through our willingness to question ourselves, learn from others, and journey together with all these ideas, that fruitfulness will begin to enrich our dialogue. In light of the many challenges currently facing our nations and societies, it seems all the more vital that Christians of different traditions should work for greater mutual understanding and deeper unity, in order that we may express and witness to the love of God in Christ more faithfully in our divided world. We hope and pray that the work of the Meissen-led Colloquium and the ongoing Meissen process may contribute in a small but significant way to our shared goal of visible unity in the Church, which we believe is God's will for his people.

Contributors

The Revd Canon Prof Mark Chapman is Vice-Principal of Ripon College Cuddesdon, Professor of the History of Modern Theology at the University of Oxford and Co-Chair of the Meissen Theological Conference.

Oberkirchenrat Frank-Dieter Fischbach is Regional Secretary for Ecumenical Relations and Ministries Abroad (Northern and Western Europe) at the Evangelical Church in Germany (EKD) and Co-Secretary of the Meissen Commission.

The Rt Revd Dr Jonathan Gibbs is Bishop of Huddersfield in the Diocese of Leeds, Lead Safeguarding Bishop for the Church of England and Co-Chair of the Meissen Commission.

The Revd Dr Matthias Grebe is the Adviser for European Church Relations at the Council for Christian Unity, Lecturer and Tutor in Theology at St Mellitus College, London, and Co-Secretary of the Meissen Commission.

Dr Miriam Haar is Study Secretary for Anglicanism and Worldwide Ecumenism at the Institute for Ecumenical Studies and Research (*Konfessionskundliches Institut*) in Bensheim.

The Ven. Dr Alex Hughes is the Archdeacon of Cambridge in the Diocese of Ely.

Professor Frances Knight is Professor Emeritus in the History of Modern Christianity at the University of Nottingham.

The Revd Canon Prof Morwenna Ludlow is Professor of Christian History and Theology at the University of Exeter and a member of the Meissen Commission.

Landesbischof Ralf Meister is Bishop of the Evangelical-Lutheran Church of Hanover, Leading Bishop of the United Evangelical Lutheran Church in Germany (VELKD) and Co-Chair of the Meissen Commission.

Professor Friederike Nüssel is Professor of Systematic Theology at the University of Heidelberg, Director of the Ecumenical Institute and Co-Chair of the Meissen Theological Conference.

Professor Bernd Oberdorfer is Professor of Systematic Theology at the University of Augsburg.

Professor Peter Scherle previously led the Theological Seminary at Herborn of the Protestant Church in Hessen and Nassau (EKHN).

Index